DEPENDENCY
AND UNDERDEVELOPMENT
IN WEST AFRICA

# INTERNATIONAL STUDIES

# IN

# SOCIOLOGY AND SOCIAL ANTHROPOLOGY

*General Editor*

## K. ISHWARAN

**VOLUME XXIX**

VICTOR C. UCHENDU (ED.)

## DEPENDENCY
## AND UNDERDEVELOPMENT
## IN WEST AFRICA

LEIDEN — E. J. BRILL — 1980

# DEPENDENCY
# AND UNDERDEVELOPMENT
# IN WEST AFRICA

EDITED BY

## VICTOR C. UCHENDU

LEIDEN — E. J. BRILL — 1980

ISBN  90 04 06170 3

# CONTENTS

# Preface

THE INSTITUTE OF AFRICAN STUDIES, University of Nigeria, Nsukka, has made its annual Workshop, which usually addresses a relevant topic of interest to the Africanist scholar and his society, an important tradition. I was privileged to be associated with the Institute and the University in the 1977-78 academic year, during my sabbatical leave from the University of Illinois. As the Institute's academic staff searched for a suitable topic for the 1978 Spring seminar—and "Workshop" is a term preferred by the Institute—we all agreed that "Dependency and Underdevelopment" should be explored. This publication grows out of the papers presented and discussed at that Workshop.

Dependency theory grew out of the Latin American development experience, an experience that is no longer an isolated one. As colonial societies in Africa and Asia joined the "club of independent states" after the World War II, the urgent political task became societal development and institutional transformation rather than decolonization. This task has not been easy. Development Plans failed to achieve their objectives and therefore crumbled under the weight of their optimistic assumptions and the growing poverty in developing nations. This in turn generated a new phase of academic self-criticism that resulted in new theories and constructive reformulation of old doctrines. Radical criticism of established doctrines led to the dependency thesis, the theme for this publication.

The central objective of the Institute was to assess what light the West African development experience would shed on the claims of dependency theory. Invitations were extended to scholars working in West African universities whose previous or current work indicated that they had an interest in the subject area. In keeping with the Institute's tradition of interdisciplinary work, many disciplines were represented at the Workshop. They included anthropology, art, economics, education, history, law, literature, philosophy, political science, religion, and sociology, among others.

Professor S. N. Nwabara, Director of the Institute, kindly assigned me the overall responsibility for preparing the manuscript for the press. Problems of collaboration in book writing over great distances are well known. Our contributing authors are now scattered over three continents. To ensure production deadline the editor assumed the role of a rewrite author for all the papers except those by Nwabara, Cookey, Ilogu, and Uchendu. While the arguments and conclusions are those of the drafting authors, the editor accepts responsibility for the final product.

African Studies Program                                     VICTOR C. UCHENDU
University of Illinois

# ACKNOWLEDGEMENT

THE PAPERS IN THIS VOLUME were originally presented and discussed at a Workshop on *Dependency and Underdevelopment in West Africa* sponsored by the Institute of African Studies at the University of Nigeria, Nsukka. The Workshop, which extended from April 24 to 27, 1978, featured more papers than could be accommodated in this publication.

We are grateful to Professor J. O. C. Ezeilo, former Vice-Chancellor of the University of Nigeria, for not only addressing the Workshop but for making the funds available in support of its expenses. Our gratitude to Professor S. N. Nwabara, Director of the Institute of African Studies at the University of Nigeria, is unequalled. He was a most hospitable host who made the welfare and comfort of the Workshop participants his personal concern. To the few Workshop participants whose papers we could not publish, we thank them for their understanding.

# Dependency and the Development Process: An Introduction

VICTOR C. UCHENDU

*University of Illinois, Urbana-Champaign, U.S.A.*

APPROXIMATELY two hundred years separate Adam Smith's, *The Wealth of Nations* and Gunnar Myrdal's, *Asian Drama.*[1] Written by master economists, the two studies are now classics—classical works which originate from the same intellectual tradition but end up with divergent prescriptions for development. As their sub-titles indicate, the two works are framed in terms of an "inquiry." Adam Smith's was "An inquiry into the wealth of nations"; and Gunnar Myrdal's "An inquiry into the poverty of nations."

*The Wealth of Nations* and *Asian Drama* symbolically call attention to two major global problems of our time: the coexistence of persistent poverty with an enormous industrial wealth in the world. What is more disturbing is the maldistribution of the world's industrial wealth.

Adam Smith wrote for a mercantile society, a new society emerging from the shell of the old, feudal society. His treatise performed the paradoxical role of both helping to smash the shell of the feudal society and also laying the firm philosophical foundations for a new capitalist age. In *Asian Drama* and other works preceding and following it, Gunnar Myrdal[2] made the question of world poverty rather than world wealth a central issue for political action and economic research. He indicts social science research for being not only opportunistic but "diplomatic, forbearing, and generally over optimistic"[3] and credits political change, particularly the political reversals of the West, which began after World War II, for the current interest in the political ecology of world poverty. He calls attention to three principal causes for this change in intellectual direction: "first, the rapid liquidation of the colonial power structure; second, the craving for development in the underdeveloped countries themselves, or rather, among that educated and articulate elite who think, speak, and act on their behalf; and third, the international tensions, especially the cold war, that have made the fate of the underdeveloped countries a matter of foreign policy concern in the developed countries."[4]

## Social Sciences and Perception of Social Problems

History, the engine of social movements, acts as the laboratory of the social sciences. As Joan Robinson phrases it, "In the social sciences, experiments are not made in laboratories but thrown up by history."[5] History creates a framework within which great thinkers and artists do their work; and works that ultimately change or challenge the accepted "world view" of a given age owe much to the history of their time. Thus it has been with Adam Smith's, *The Wealth of Nations* and with Karl Marx's, *The Capital*. It is the breakdown of the market economy in the great slump of the 1930s that led to the Keynesian revolution—a revolution in economic thought that has now spent its force and is of limited relevance when applied to the economic problems of late developing countries.

The Keynesian revolution is a limited revolution. Far from creating a radically new "economic world," Keynes simply revised the image with which the capitalist world might be viewed. Breaking away from the notion that the growth in the wealth of a nation, like that of a single family, depends on saving, Keynes argued that:

> ...In a modern capitalist economy, accumulation is not controlled by household saving but by the investments of profit-seeking firms. In the situation of the slump, investment was low because prospects for profits were weak and uncertain. Because investment was low, employment was low and incomes were low. To accept this point of view meant to admit that there is an inherent defect in the *laissez faire* system, that the concept of a natural tendency to equilibrium is misconceived and that household saving is a consequence rather than a cause of capital accumulation.[6]

The social sciences are led by the historical process. Seldom do they lead to new radical social perspectives. Their greatest strength lies in the revision of existing images of the world. In his very readable book, *The Impact of the Social Sciences,* Kenneth Boulding[7] argues that while the rate of increase of the operating body of knowledge available to a society is important to its development, nevertheless, for a new knowledge to facilitate development, it must contribute to the constant revision of "images of the world" held by a changing society, and this is best achieved through refined observation and testing. In a general sweep of human history and cultural development, Boulding calls attention to three epochs in human social development, each of which revised the existing "image of the world" and thus created a new image.[8] Much of man's recorded history is marked by "folk knowledge" which antedates civilization and still manifests itself in many areas of contemporary life: in the running of our domestic life and in carrying on basic interaction with our friends, strangers, friends and foes. The invention and use of writing, which gave birth to "classical civilization" around 3000 B.C., brought with it the knowledge system which Kenneth Boulding characterizes as the "literary knowledge process." Man entered the "science age" only about three centuries ago, and thus created the most flexible knowledge system—the "scientific process"—the most efficient tool so far developed by man for constant revision of our image of the world. Kenneth Boulding attributes to the "scientific process":

> the increase in knowledge which...has doubled the span of human life, has carried man into space, has explored the whole surface of the earth, has released enormous sources of energy,

has created wholly new materials, and has created an enormous increase in productivity and affluence. It has increased per capita incomes in some parts of the world at least twenty times in two hundred years; it has also given us fantastic weapons, enormous insecurity in the international system, death-dealing modes of transport, an almost unmanageable population explosion, and the neurotic personality of our time.[9]

The great ideas produced by the social sciences are shaped by the historical process. This is understandable because the social sciences are part of the social system which helps to shape and produce them. As the dynamics of the social system work themselves out, the direction of social sciences changes accordingly. Examples from the political economies of Western Europe come readily to mind. The eighteenth century mercantilism produced Adam Smith's doctrine of "natural liberty" and the theories of division of labour and free exchange and free markets which it spawned. So also did demographic pressure and low industrial wages produce Malthus. While Marx and Engels reacted against feudal Germany and paleo-industrial Manchester, Keynes was the creature of the Great Depression of the 1930s. Dependency theory, which was inspired by the economic experiences of Latin America, has become a Third World theoretical response to "growth without development" and "persistent poverty" which post-colonial societies inherited.

If every age in history has its own preoccupation, the post-colonial society is certainly preoccupied with the problem of inequality—inequality among nations and within nations—the various manifestations of inequality, its root causes and how to eradicate it. The visible manifestation of inequality is poverty. The poverty of nations is not a new condition in human history. What is new is that the "poverty of nations" became politically visible about the same time that poverty became politically unacceptable. Our new "world image" has rendered traditional ideas and theories of the origin of poverty obsolete. Poverty is no longer accepted as the result of individual failure; and the view that it is caused by race or geography has been rightly discredited. An alternative proposition suggests that poverty in its widest sense is caused by the way society is organized.

Our understanding of the real causes of world poverty and unequal development has been limited by what Susanne Langer calls "generative ideas—the wealth of formulative notions with which the mind meets experiences."[10] Observing that "most new discoveries are sudden-seen things that were always there," she likens a generative idea to:

> ...a light that illuminates presences which simply had no form for us before the light fell on them. Yet it is the most natural and appropriate thing in the world for a new terminology to have a vogue that crowds out everything else for a while. A word that everyone snaps up...the "Open Sesame" of some new positive science. The sudden vogue of such a key-idea is due to the fact that all sensitive and active minds turn at once to exploiting it; we try it in every connection, for every purpose, experiment with possible stretches of its strict meaning, with generalizations and derivatives. When we become familiar with the new idea our expectations do not outrun its actual uses so far, and then its unbalanced popularity is over. We settle down to the problems that it has really generated, and these become the characteristic issues of our time.[11]

Whether the dependency hypothesis is a *grande idée*, ''a generative idea,'' in Susanne Langer's terminology, which promises to ''resolve so many fundamental problems at once that [it] also promises to...resolve all fundamental problems, clarify all obscure issues'' will be revealed by time.[12] One thing is clear. Dependency theory has focussed attention on a major issue of international proportion which can no longer be ignored—an issue that was well documented before the dependency hypothesis became popular.

## Dependency and Underdevelopment: Evolution of a Theory

The central idea which governs dependency theory is the fact of global inequality. Dependency theory asserts that a country's position in an international system of dependent or unequal exchange and political control conditions its development strategies and achievements. Dependency analysts point to the pattern of unequal exchange among nations and the social stratification that results from it in support of this thesis.

The complex relationship between social inequality and economic progress leads naturally to many interpretations. With reference to the global society, the pattern of social and economic changes in poor countries, particularly their economic performance relative to that of advanced, industrial societies since the end of World War II, has led to a re-evaluation of the earlier theories of the role of dominant systems in the development process. Explanations of how relations of international dependency, which implies national subordination for poor countries, have fostered international exploitation by rich nations on the one hand, and domestic parasitism and exploitation by the national elite on the other, are central to dependency analyses. Fernando Cardoso, one of the pioneers of the dependency thesis, claims that the *dependentistas* had two principal objectives. First, to provide a revisionist tool of Marxist analysis that makes sense in terms of Latin American development history. In his own words, ''A study of the history of ideas in the twentieth century would show that each generation of critical intellectuals seeks to revive Marxism with a new breadth of life. Studies of dependency constitute part of this constantly renewed effort to re-establish a tradition of analysis of economic structures and structures of domination.'' Second, ''dependency analyses in the years 1965-68 were preoccupied much less with the external conditioning of Latin American economies, than with the development of a type of analysis that could grasp the political alliances, the ideologies and the movement structures within the dependent countries.''[13]

The two objectives which Cardoso set for dependency theory have been exceeded. Dependency theory has become not only a tool of social analysis but an explicit ideology as well as a programme of political and economic action. A. G. Hopkins tells us the reason.

> ...Since Western capitalism has, so far, failed to solve the problems of the Third World and is itself experiencing a profound crisis, it is not surprising that the main drive behind the current revival of history comes from a radical pessimism which draws its inspiration,

though not always its teaching, from Marx. The new history has a clear focus and commitment. It is centred on the dependency thesis...(in the argument) that capitalism had retarded the independent development of the Third World...The fortunes of the dependent countries are decided by the dominant industrial powers, and the expansion of the capitalist centre is assisted by the transfer of surplus value from the periphery."[14]

There may be argument about how far the rich, industrial countries exploit the poor countries. On the question of the proportion of the population in poor countries who are in poverty, there is little disagreement. On the basis of cross-section evidence covering the period 1950-63, Adelman concludes that "the primary impact of economic development on income distribution is, on the average, to decrease both the absolute and the relative incomes of the poor." She states emphatically that, "not only is there no automatic trickle-down of the benefits of development; on the contrary, the development process leads typically to a trickle-up in favor of the middle classes and the rich. The poorest segments of the population typically benefit from economic growth only when the government plays an important economic role." She concludes, "economic structure, not the level or rate of economic growth, is the basic determinant of pattern of income distribution. The price of economic equity is high: a necessary condition for its achievement is radical structural change."[15] Although David Morawetz prefers time series data to cross section evidence as a basis for drawing conclusions on the comparative performance of international economies, his analysis, covering the period 1950-75, ends with three uncomfortable conclusions. The growth performance of developing countries during this period is marked by "rapid average growth rate, the wide diversity of experience, and the increasing disparity between richer and poorer developing countries."[16]

The central problem in dependency is not the rate of economic growth as such but the factors which condition this growth rate. Furthermore, the *dependentistas* are more interested in social development broadly conceived than in economic growth.

Dependency theory has its critics,[17] its defenders,[18] and its chief theoreticians.[19] Critics have come from the right and the left; and since "no unified theory of dependency yet exists,"[20] a variety of theoretical orientations have emerged, attracting criticism from a variety of ideological positions. Two traditions of the theory of dependency are usually distinguished, and they vary in analytical approach and policy recommendations.[21] The earliest tradition of the theory, led by economists at the Economic Commission for Latin America (ECLA), was structuralist in perspective and nationalist in ideology. Another tradition came from a Marxist perspective which insisted on class analysis and socialism as a matter of ideological commitment but unequivocally upheld national independence as an anti-Stalinist posture.

Methodological criticism of dependency theory has come from both the right and the left. Hopkins is in sympathy with any development theory which does not ignore the lessons of the past, particularly the contribution of economic historians. However, he criticizes dependency theory "for producing an orthodoxy some way in advance of the evidence needed to validate it.'' He concedes that the theory ''can claim a new terminology and a shift in [theoretical] focus,'' but does not yet ''constitute a novel paradigm'' nor has it resolved the important problem of periodization.[22] For instance, in the context of African studies what is the pre-dependence period? O'Brien criticizes the theory from the perspective of the methodology of positivist social science. Arguing that ''theories of dependency may seem at best trivial or irrelevant and at worst politcal slogans wrapped up as a theory,'' O'Brien takes issue with a methodology that does not ''study the dynamics of a society...at an empirical level [but] abstractions which do not exist in a pure form in the real world have to be made and the concrete approached via 'successive approximations'.''[23]

David Ray raises a telling conceptual and substantive criticism of the dependency theory. He argues, rather logically and convincingly, that dependency is not a dichotomous variable, that the choice is not between dependency and non-dependency because non-dependency does not and cannot exist in an interdependent world. With Chinese accusations of Soviet imperialism and hegemony in mind, and Eastern European dependence on Soviet Union as an important example, Ray takes issue with the dependency doctrine that the ambition and capacity to build and exploit satellite relationships is exclusively a capitalist orientation. He writes:

> Soviet economic imperialism has been no less a reality than the capitalist variety. Indeed, there is a striking similarity between the economic dependence which has been imposed upon Latin America by the United States and the economic dependence which has been imposed upon Eastern Europe by the Soviet Union.''[24]

Gilbert answers Ray's criticism by claiming that socialist dependency is not a functional equivalence of capitalist dependency. He argues that capitalist dependency results from ''blind economic forces by highly developed capitalism'' while socialist dependency results from ''the policy of a particular regime in a particular time period,'' implying that the former is parasitic, endemic and exploitative and the latter is variable and transitional.[25] Gilbert does not sound entirely convincing when he asserts that socialist dependency is essentially political in character, ''the result of policy, of dogma, and of circumstances which allowed a privileged bureaucracy to usurp political power...[and therefore] does not carry with it economic consequences.''[26]

If the dependency thesis means anything, it must guarantee political freedom to the Third World countries—freedom from political interference by both the socialist East and capitalist West—as the basis for self-reliant development.

## Dependency and the West African Experience

Dependency theory developed as a new, radical interpretation of Latin American economic and social development. Its early tradition tried to provide a ''definitive refutation, not only of Marxists who distort historical realities, but also of bourgeois liberals who are apologists for the dependence of Latin American countries on the metropolis."[27] It is not surprising that the theory has been attacked from both sides: by the left for neglecting the Marxist traditional orthodoxy; and by the right for identifying the "wrong enemy," careless use of Marxist theory and faulty methodology.

Because of the inherent flexibility of its terminology, dependency theory is gradually winning some friends in Africa where the dependency theme has been best popularized by Samir Amin and Walter Rodney.[28] Except for Marxists, Africanist writers who use the dependency theme are rather eclectic in their orientations. Colonialism, Neo-colonialism, and Multi-national Corporations appear as the "immediate enemy" in this literature.[29]

In his contribution to this publication, Uchendu summarizes the claims of dependency theory under six propositions:

First, underdevelopment results from dependence.

Second, underdevelopment results mainly from exploitation—the exploitation of the weak by the strong.

Third, development and underdevelopment are dialectically linked, the former impoverishes the latter while the latter enriches the former.

Fourth, underdevelopment is not just the product of local or national history; it is the product of a global, imperial history.

Fifth, underdevelopment is not caused by archaic social structure and traditional institutional arrangements, but by piratical advanced capitalism.

Sixth, there is only one cure for underdevelopment: de-satellization and socialism.

Dependency theory, like all paradigms, should be treated like "scaffoldings, good for a single building only, and needing to be scrapped when the movements of history and of thought present us with different problems and different ways of perceiving problems."[30] What does the West African historical experience suggest? Cookey approaches this question against the back-ground of Nigerian colonial history. He calls attention to the "unique colonial experience of each underdeveloped country" and the necessity to take into consideration their substantial diversity before we generalize the effects of colonialism on economic achievement of dependent nations. While recognizing the "indirect benefits" of colonial rule in Nigeria, it is Cookey's central thesis that colonialism put the Nigerian society and economy on a kind of "receivership" by denying Nigerian peoples an effective voice in determining their own future.

Cookey draws no firm conclusion in favour or against the central proposition of dependency theory as such. He implies, however, that political independence, supported by abundant economic resources in the hands of a nationalist elite could lead to development. He concludes, "It is not without interest and significance that the prospects of Nigeria's development has considerably brightened since her membership of the Oil Producing and Exporting Countries (OPEC) which has broken the price control hitherto imposed by the developed countries."

The paper by Sonaike and Olowoporoku attempts a redefinition of the meaning of "economic dependence," using the historical approach. Following a review, a critique and the rejection of both the orthodox and the radical schools of thought on the subject, they propose a new definition of economic dependence that takes into consideration the necessity to maintain some fair level of interdependence in the fields of trade and technology. They emphasize that "the fact that a nation depends on foreign trade to raise or maintain its living standards would not make it economically dependent provided it possesses a competitive technology and is not politically dominated by outsiders."

In their attempt to provide a new perspective on the concept of dependence, Sonaike and Olowoporoku have emphasized the notion of relative dependence. In their view, the real world does not consist entirely of capitalist exploiters and their dependent satellite states. Rather, they recognize three structural configurations: "The super-dominant economies of the advanced capitalist and socialist countries; the emerging sub-dominant economies; and the perpetually aid-dependent economies, the so called "poorest of the poor" nations." The implication of this structural distinction is that while some forms of dependency are direct, other forms are indirect. They conclude by asserting that in order to eliminate dependency "it will be necessary that the periphery be in complete control of political power and its leaders be in a position to redirect their external orientation."

Sullivan presents a case study of the Nigerian economy in his attempt to assess what it might reveal in terms of the claims of structural dependency. He finds "evidence of strongly dualistic structures" in the Nigerian economy—a dualism that reveals itself in income distribution between the rural and urban areas; between the unskilled urban and rural labourer; and between the regions in Nigeria. His analysis shows that the nationalist elite can act in the national interest and against the interest of monopoly capital and world imperialism. He asks, "Why did Nigeria suddenly decide to reduce the degree of dependency on foreign capitalism when the composition of its ruling class was not vastly different from that of the preceding decade?" He finds the answer partly in the emergence of petroleum as the new engine of economic development in Nigeria, and partly in political pressure.

Capital is not the only basis for dependency. In developing countries, the dearth of high level managerial skills and limited technological capacity fosters other forms of dependency. The Nigerian economy exemplifies this problem. "A substantial evidence exists to support the thesis that dependency on expatriate, executive management will continue for some time to come mainly due to the policies of firms who appear to deliberately avoid the process of Nigerianization." Sullivan finds the solution to this problem in a forceful government action, which can express itself in the secondment or transfer of "top flight Nigerian executives from the public sector to the private sector"—a solution which is only realistic in corporations where the Nigerian government has a substantial interest.

While recognizing that Nigeria is "an integral component of peripheral countries," Sullivan does not see socialist solution as the appropriate strategy for Nigeria. He cautions that "programs and policies which are designed to disengage a poor country from dependency should not necessarily lead it away from the path of interdependency." He concludes, "because of its enormously rich natural resources, Nigeria can afford to disengage its economy from the burdens of the colonial past and build an economic system which is committed to the principles of fair income distribution while providing enough incentives for its entrepreneurs."

Development and underdevelopment are ideologically rooted. Nwala examines the role of ideology in the Nigerian development process. Adopting a neo-Marxist frame of reference, he argues that ideologies are both "class centred" and relative to their particular social reality. Viewing Nigeria as an ideologically dependent country, Nwala argues that the country can only perpetuate a neo-colonial structure of external domination with its present reformist economic strategies. How will Nigeria regain its ideological autonomy? Nwala's prescriptions are predictable: "For Nigeria to regain autonomy over her economic, social, and political life, she must first break her ties with world monopoly capitalism in which she is only a convenient appendage."

Kodjo tackles a wider issue than ideology—the problem of cultural independence for West Africa. Arguing that we cannot understand dependency if we ignore its cultural content, Kodjo illustrates how the West African cultural values have been eroded by the ideology and practices of colonial education. He asserts that "education is never politically and ideologically neutral," that it is the task of a colonial educational system to make its subjects subservient and the responsibility of a nationalist educational system to lead its people to cultural freedom.

Although the case study on the history of colonial education presented by Kodjo is derived from the French West African experience, nevertheless, his insights have broad implications. He recognizes the "image" warfare between the capitalist West and socialist East "for the control of the minds of developing countries" and finds that a properly informed and ideologically oriented educational system can act as a powerful countervailing force for maintaining the cultural integrity of West Africa. Lamenting the fact that West African cultural emancipation lags far behind its formal political emancipation, Kodjo reminds us that "the laws governing political emancipation and educational emancipation are not the same." He calls for "a centripetally oriented educational strategy" as the only instrument capable of decolonizing the minds of the West African peoples, getting them to accept their local realities, and winning for them cultural freedom.

On the theme of dependency and cultural processes, Uchendu employs the theory of cultural dynamics to examine both the limits of dependency theory and the claims of cultural autonomy and cultural convergence. He notes the two paradoxical facts of contemporary history: a world divided by the harsh realities of social and economic inequality and the memory of past, and in places, continuing exploitation and racial and ethnic injustic; and a world more interdependent and culturally more convergent in the 1970s than in any other comparable period in man's recent history. Hypothesizing that cultural convergence is likely to continue, even if politically restricted to a few institutional sectors, Uchendu wonders whether similar structural choices—capitalism or socialism, for instance—are likely to replicate their respective cultural contents in West Africa. Uchendu's hypothesis is prompted by an apparent cultural irony detectable from dependency theory. If the choice is between capitalism and socialism, can this choice be made without compromising that African cultural autonomy that all contributors to this symposium consider important to protect and preserve?

Uchendu does not see cultural process as that simple. He distinguishes between *assimilative* and *integrative* convergent cultures, suggesting that cultural convergence of the integrative type is culturally less costly, in the exchange or interactive process, than the assimilative type. He concludes that dependency theory ignores interdependence and the probable benefits flowing from it.

The theme of interdependence in the context of regional institutional autonomy is explored by Aghaji and Ilogu; and with special reference to the Nigerian law, Nwabara examines the "dependency effect" of the British legal system on the Nigerian law ways.

The emergence of political independence brought into focus the economic limitations of national boundaries which West African states inherited from colonial rule. In a region where most of the states are poorly and unevenly endowed by nature and therefore externally aid-dependent, the strategies recommended by dependency theorists do not make much sense. Aghaji searches for a regional institution which will help West African states to diversify their dependence and he finds it in the ECOWAS—Economic Council of West African States. It is his view that for the ECOWAS to become "an instrument of economic independence in the West African region," there must be a political will to sustain the institution and the willingness on the part of its member states to surrender some of their national sovereignty to the regional authority.

Religion cannot be ignored in any serious discussion of cultural and institutional autonomy in West Africa. This is because "exported religions", a phrase Ilogu applies to Islam and Christianity, "carry with them cultural values, concepts, and world views which are foreign to West Africa." He asserts that the conflict between African traditional institutions and the "exported religions," particularly Christianity, has made indigenization a practical necessity. He illustrates the process of indigenizing the Christian rites and ideas with case studies from Nigeria and Ghana, implying that West African societies can, in fact, accept these religious exports as needed and functional "imports". Ilogu recognizes that we live in an interdependent cultural system—a theme Uchendu explored in his thesis on cultural convergence. He indicates why, in a culturally interdependent world, religious ideas cannot be entirely independent. "Human beings have a common ideational heritage," he observes, and it is this heritage "which makes it possible for an idea expressed in one language to be interpreted in or communicated to another language."

Our common ideational heritage does not always lead us to the same institutional path. The institution of the law is a good example of man's divergent responses to the common problem of maintaining order in society. As in eduction and religion, West Africa is also heir to a plural heritage in law. Nwabara discusses the history and the cultural dynamics of Nigeria's "Received Law"—the English Common Law and the Islamic Law of the Maliki School. He traces systematically the erosion of the Nigerian traditional legal culture as a result of politically imposed, alien legal institutions. He observes that the "Repugnancy doctrine" used to test the acceptability of the Nigerian customary law put the customary law in bondage. He is disturbed that legal reforms have ignored the philosophical foundation on which the "Received Law" in Nigeria is based. He concludes that planning for national independence "must be rooted in the people's culture in all its ramifications—the indigenous law not excepted."

## Concluding Remarks

The contributors to this publication addressed varying subject areas which touch on the West African development experience. Dependency theory provided a common theoretical frame of reference. As we expected, the responses were eclectic. All the contributors recognized that colonialism and its institutions imposed upon West Africa structural and cultural patterns which foster dependency. There is a recognition, too, that there are various forms of dependency. There is, however, a sharp division of opinion on the strategy for achieving independence, even though there is unanimity on the necessity for an independent West African region. The division of opinion was partly ideological and partly due to the economic realities in West Africa.

The West African region, like other parts of Africa, is not evenly endowed by nature. Nigeria, for instance, dominates the region in population and proven mineral resources. Her strategy for disengaging from dependence naturally must be different from strategies which other states within the region might consider appropriate. Like other regions in Africa, the West African states function within inherited colonial boundaries. A few are large by African standards and many are small; and some of the large states are in semi-arid belts, with limited resources, including rainfall, which is indispensable for the rainfed agriculture practised in the region.

No matter their size, population or natural resource endowment, the West African countries share similar experiences of a region whose institutions were shaped by colonialism and continually activated and mediated by the ex-colonial powers. Education, religion, the economy, and the law are among the institutions which have not lost their colonial character and they still manifest the external dependency of West Africa.

West Africa is not only externally dependent; it also maintains a high degree of interdependence with the world system in a limited number of spheres. This is the basis for its growing cultural convergence—a process that is likely to continue as long as West Africa maintains active interaction with the world system. Although some of our contributors see revolution as the only strategy for achieving independence for West Africa, the elite in power naturally think otherwise. They are following a strategy of "diversified dependency" as a stage toward national and regional autonomy.

The thesis that "the rich 'underdevelop' the poor and that international integration leads to national disintegration [because] dominant groups in the developing countries...are subservient to the international system of inequality, conformity and underdevelopment [which] they perpetuate"[31] ignores one fundamental political fact in West Africa: the countervailing effects of nationalism. West African states are very nationalistic. This should not be surprising, given the recency of their formal political independence. What is rather surprising is that dependency theorists would expect Third World countries to detach themselves from the international system whose many arenas provide them opportunities to demonstrate, even if only symbolically, their newly won independence. Given the prolonged political and cultural agony of the Black man, is it a sensible strategy for African countries to trade their present status of "multiple dependency" for what they perceive as a possible "monopoly political control" by one dominant ideological system that might end up in total dependency? This is a practical challenge to the anti-nationalist but pro-socialist dependency theorist.

BIBLIOGRAPHY

AMIN, SAMIR, *Unequal Development.* Sussex, England, 1976.
——. *Accumulation on a World Scale: A Critique of the Theory of Underdevelopment.* New York: Monthly Review Press, 1974.
——. *Neocolonialism in West Africa.* Penguin African Library, 1973.
BATH RICHARD C. and JAMES, D. D. "Dependency Analysis of Latin America: Some Criticisms, Some Suggestions." *Latin American Research Review* 11 (1976):3-53.
BONAPARTE, T. H. "Multi-national Corporations and Culture in Liberia." *The American Journal of Economics and Sociology* 38 (1979):237-51.
BOULDING, KENNETH E. *The Impact of Social Sciences.* Rutgers University Press, 1966.
BRETT, E. A. *Colonialism and Underdevelopment in East Africa: The Politics of Economic Change 1919-1939.* New York: Nok Publishers, 1973.
CARDOSO, FERNANDO H. "The Consumption of Dependency Theory in the United States." *Latin American Research Review* XII, 3 (1977):7-24.
CHILCOTE, RONALD H. "Dependency: A Critical Synthesis of the Literature." *Latin American Perspectives,* I, 1 (1974):4-27.
——. "A Question of Dependency." *Latin American Research Review* XII, 2 (1978):55-68.
FERNÁNDEZ, RAÚL A. and OCAMPO, JOSÉ F. "The Latin American Revolution: A Theory of Imperialism, Not Dependence." *Latin American Perspectives* I, 1 (1974):30-61.
FRANK, GUNDER. "Dependence is Dead, Long Live Dependence and Class Struggle: A Reply to Critics." *Latin American Perspectives* I, 1 (1974):87-106.
GEERTZ, CLIFFORD. *The Interpretation of Cultures.* London: Hutchinson, 1975.

GILBERT, GUY J. "Socialism and Dependency." *Latin American Perspectives* I, 1 (1974):107-23.

HOPKINS, A. G. "Clio-Antics: A Horoscope for African Economic History." In *African Studies Since 1945: A Tribute to Basil Davidson.* Edited by C. Fyfe. London: Longmans, 1976.

LANGER, SUSAN K. *Philosophy in a New Key: A Study in the Symbolism of Reason, Rite and Art.* New York: Mentor Books, 1962.

MORAWETZ, DAVID. *Twenty-five Years of Economic Development: 1950 to 1975.* Baltimore: The Johns Hopkins University Press, 1977.

MYRDAL, GUNNAR *Rich Lands and Poor Lands: The Road to World Prosperity.* New York: Harper, 1957.

——. *Asian Drama: An Inquiry Into the Poverty of Nations.* New York: Twentieth Century Fund, 1968.

O'BRIEN, PHILIP J. "A Critique of Latin American Theories of Dependency." In *Beyond the Sociology of Development: Economy and Society in Latin America and Africa.* Edited by Iva Oxaal, et al. London: Routledge and Kegan Paul, 1975, pp. 7-27.

RAY, DAVID "The Dependency Model of Latin American Under-Development: Three Basic Fallacies." *Journal of Inter-American and World Affairs* XV, 1 (1973):4-20.

RIESMAN, DAVID *Abundance For What?* New York: Doubleday and Company, Inc. 1964.

ROBINSON, JOAN "Michal Kalecki on the Economics of Capitalism." *Oxford Bulletin of Economics and Statistics* 39 (1977):7-17.

RODNEY, W. *How Europe Underdeveloped Africa.* Dar-es-Salaam: Tanzania Publishing House, 1973.

SMITH, ADAM *The Wealth of Nations: An Inquiry Into the Nature and Causes.* New York: The Modern Library, 1937.

## NOTES

1   Smith, The Wealth of Nations (New York: The Modern Library, 1937); Myrdal, *Asian Drama: An Inquiry into the Poverty of Nations* (New York: Twentieth Century Fund, 1968).

2   Myrdal, *Rich Lands and Poor Lands: The Road to World Prosperity* (New York: Harper, 1957); *The Challenge of World Poverty: A World Anti-Poverty Program in Outline* (New York: Vintage Books, 1971).

3   Myrdal, *The Challenge of World Poverty,* p. 8.

4   Ibid., p. 6.

5   Robinson, "Michal Kalecki on the Economics of Capitalism," *Oxford Bulletin of Economics and Statistics* 39 (1977):7.

6   Ibid., p. 7-8.

7   Kenneth E. Boulding, *The Impact of Social Sciences* (Rutgers University Press, 1966).

8   Ibid., pp. 7-9.

9   Ibid., p. 10.

10   Langer, *Philosophy in a New Key* (New York: Mentor Books, 1962), p. 19.

11   Ibid., pp. 19, 31.

12   Geertz, *The Interpretation of Cultures* (London: Hutchinson, 1975), p. 3.

13   Cardoso, "The Consumption of Dependency Theory in the United States," *Latin American Research Review* xii, 3 (1977):10-12.

14   Hopkins, "Clio-Antics: A Horoscope for African Economic History," in *African Studies Since 1945,* Fyfe (ed.), (London: Longmans, 1976), pp. 32-3.

15   Adelman, "Development Economics: A Reassessment of Goals," *The American Economic Review* LXV, 2 (1975):302-9.

16   Morawetz, *Twenty-five Years of Economic Development: 1950 to 1975* (Baltimore: The Johns Hopkins University Press, 1977), pp. 12, 42-3.

17   Fernandez and Ocampo, "The Latin American Revolution: A Theory of Imperialism, Not Dependence," *Latin American Perspectives* I, 1 (1974):30-61; A. Hopkins, "Clio-Antics"; Bath and James, "Dependency Analysis of Latin America: Some Criticisms, Some Suggestions," *Latin American Research Review* 11 (1976):3-53; Ray, "The Dependency Model of

Latin American Underdevelopment: Three Basic Fallacies," *Journal of Inter-American and World Affairs* XV (1973):4-20; O'Brien, "A Critique of Latin American Theories of Dependency," in *Beyond the Sociology of Development,* Oxaal, Barnett and Booth (eds.), (London: Routledge and Kegan Paul, 1975), pp. 7-27.

18  Frank, "Dependence is Dead, Long Live Dependence and Class Struggle: A Reply to Critics," *Latin American Perspectives* I, 1 (1974):87-106.

19  Chilcote, "Dependency: A Critical Synthesis of the Literature," *Latin American Perspectives* I, 1 (1974):4-28; "A Question of Dependency," *Latin American Research Review* XIII, 2 (1978):55-68; Gilbert, "Socialism and Dependency," *Latin American Perspectives* I, 1 (1974): 107-23.

20  Chilcote, "A Question of Dependency," p. 55; "Dependency: A Critical Synthesis,", p. 7.

21  Bath and James, "Dependency Analysis," pp. 6-11; O'Brien, "A Critique," p. 11; Chilcote, "A Question of Dependency," p. 61.

22  Hopkins, "Clio-Antics," pp. 33-5.

23  O'Brien, "A Critique of Latin American Theories," p. 11.

24  Ray, "The Dependency Model," p. 8.

25  Gilbert, "Socialism and Dependency," p. 108.

26  Ibid., p. 120.

27  Fernandez and Ocampo, "The Latin American Revolution," p. 31.

28  Samir Amin, *Unequal Development* (Sussex, England, 1976); *Accumulation on a World Scale: A Critique of the Theory of Underdevelopment* (New York: Monthly Review Press, 1974); *Neocolonialism in West Africa* (Penguin African Library, 1973); W. Rodney, *How Europe Underdeveloped Africa* (Dar-es-Salaam: Tanzania Publishing House, 1973).

29  Brett, *Colonialism and Underdevelopment in East Africa* (New York: Nok Publishers, 1973).

30  Riesman, *Abundance For What?* (New York: Doubleday, 1964), p. 593.

31  Bonaparte, "Multi-national Corporations and Culture in Liberia," *The American Journal of Economics and Sociology* 38, 3 (1979):328.

PART I

THE HISTORICAL AND ECONOMIC DIMENSIONS
OF DEPENDENCY

# Colonialism and the Process of Underdevelopment in Nigeria

*A Review*

S. J. S. COOKEY

*Department of Africana Studies, Rutgers University, New Brunswick, U.S.A.*

In 1860 THE BRITISH ANNEXED LAGOS aṣ a Crown Colony and thus began a process of territorial expansion which resulted in the birth of the British protectorate christened Nigeria at the end of the nineteenth century. Britain was to exercise sovereign power over Nigeria until 1960 when the inhabitants were granted independence. At that time Nigeria was classified as one of the underdeveloped (also developing or less developed) countries of the world, a status from which she is yet to escape.

## Underdevelopment: The Meaning and the Process

Most scholars are agreed on the meaning and implications of underdevelopment. It is characterized by low per capita production, a dependence for export (foreign exchange) earnings on one or a few primary products or raw materials which are subject to price fluctuations beyond the control of the producers, reliance on the import of manufactured consumer goods, and a static or declining standard of living in relation to the industrialized countries. Almost all the contemporary developing countries have been subjected to colonial domination. International concern for the plight of those countries classified as underdeveloped has generated considerable debate on the origins and character of underdevelopment. In particular, many have sought to confront the question whether colonialism was the primary cause of underdevelopment or whether it enhanced the chances of development.

Some have argued that colonialism was not a negative force. Although it denied the colonized people the initiative to determine their own future and map out their own economic options, it also laid the foundations for the emergence of a new political order and the possibility of an economic transformation. They point out that the concept of modernization (developed by Western social scientists) is rooted in the colonial experience. Within Africa, for example, the "New Imperialism" was responsible for the conglomeration of hundreds of hitherto autonomous ethnic groups within new and often more rational territorial groups which came to conceive of themselves as nation-states. Although the institutional and infrastructural developments that took place might have been motivated by the selfish interests of the colonizers, they did stimulate change in the direction that made general economic development potentially possible. Equally important, the cultural contact between colonizer and colonized directly or indirectly released a set of ideas and knowledge which would generate a greater awareness of the possibilities for revolutionary change. Thus, far from contributing to underdevelopment, the colonial rulers, for the most part, successfully shouldered the "White Man's Burden" by putting an end to intertribal warfare, improving social welfare, introducing new technology, increasing production, and generally raising the standard of living of the colonized. For these scholars, then, the colonial period was a stage, even a necessary stage, in the progress of the colonized people towards economic development.[1]

Other scholars have agreed with Karl Marx that the consequence of colonialism was the transformation of "one part of the globe into a chiefly agricultural field of production, for supplying the other part which remains a chiefly industrial field."[2] It also marked, according to Peter Worsley, "the consolidation of the world as a single social system" characterized by the polarization of nations, or as Gustavo Lagos called it, "a system of social stratification" between the rich and the poor, between the industrialized and the underdeveloped nations."[3] This transformation was undertaken by forcibly depriving the colonized people of their independence and by creating an institutional framework which fostered the primary economic objectives of the colonizers. Order and social stability was of crucial concern. Thus colonial governments, where they could not govern directly, either preserved or appointed indigenous rulers whose interests coincided with theirs and ensured the maintenance of the colonial status quo. Educational institutions were established to train a cadre of subordinate officials to supplement the hierarchy of expatriate officials that dominated the colonial system. Medical science and technology and improved nutrition and sanitation helped to reduce the death rate, improved the birth rate, and stimulated the growth of population thus ensuring an adequate supply of the labour force. Improvements in transport and communication were undertaken to facilitate the movement of export produce rather than the strengthening of the domestic economy. Tariff arrangements bound the colonial economy closely to the metropolis in what Gunnar Myrdal has called "enforced bilateralism" which excluded outside competition thereby restricting the market options of the dependent territory and worsening its terms of trade.

The problem with these general statements from the opposite sides of the argument is that they take little account of the unique colonial experience of each underdeveloped country. The substantial diversity among these territories is obvious enough. They vary enormously in size and population; some are totally dependent on a single crop or mineral for economic growth which makes them more vulnerable than those with diversified natural resources; some have well-entrenched "dual" economies (as between the modern and traditional sectors) while others are somewhat more integrated; some have the manpower necessary to operate a modern economy while others are lacking in this respect. Because of differences, it seems appropriate to examine each territory in greater detail against the background of the theoretical generalizations which have been made.

## Nigeria: A Case Study

The case of Nigeria is particularly interesting because with an area of about 357,000 square miles and a population approximating to 80 million, it falls among the twenty largest countries in the world. Although the configuration of its boundaries has been influenced by the pre-colonial experience of individual ethnic groups, such as the rise of the Sokoto Caliphate and the Yoruba civil wars, it was ultimately the diplomatic negotiations between Britain, France and Germany that determined the territorial limits of Nigeria. Within these limits, a large number of ethnic groups, varying in size and culture, were brought under a single administration by 1914. Few would argue that this action created a potentially viable economic unit or market with tremendous human and natural resources which was capable of developing a sound economy.

However, some would contest that, under colonialism, it was impossible to embark on policies which would guarantee such an outcome. The indigenous population had been deprived of an effective voice in determining their future. The administrative structure erected by Britain was meant to serve imperial interests. The colonial governor was an autocrat responsible only to the Colonial Secretary in Downing Street, London, and as long as he balanced the budget and avoided costly wars with the local inhabitants, which would arouse liberal opinion, he was left undisturbed in his domain until he had served out his term. As is well-known, the first governor of Northern Nigeria, Sir Frederick (later Lord) Lugard, introduced a system of local administration which became famous as Indirect Rule. Its outcome was to incorporate local rulers, confirmed in office by the governor, into the colonial system and by supporting them, he succeeded in making them subservient to the wishes of the alien regime. The system gave rise to a number of petty despots whose interests became bound up with those of the British administration. In the event, the indigenous political institutions, far from being preserved, became warped. The problem of establishing a system of local administration which would cater to the needs of the masses has proved intractable even since.

Considerable debate has raged over the characteristic features of the system as it compared with French practice in neighbouring colonies. One major difference was the degree of autonomy which the British, unlike the French, gave to the traditional rulers. What is more pertinent, however, is the fact that the authority thus conferred was retained only as long as the traditional rulers loyally executed official British policy. In particular, they not only had to maintain law and order but also to collect local taxes which were meant to goad the people into either the wage economy or the production of cash crops required by foreign firms.

Thus, both at the central and local levels of the administration, colonial rule in Nigeria, prior to World War II, failed to establish institutions which would serve the interests of the governed. Indeed, during the high noon of colonialism which might be said to have extended from 1914 to 1939, the idea of Nigeria emerging as a nation-state was hardly contemplated. Cleavages existed between the British and their subjects, between the Muslim provinces of the North and the non-Muslim westernized elements of the South, and between local rulers and their people. Such fragmentation of authority and interests only confirmed Nigeria as a "geographical expression" with consequences which would ultimately lead to civil war and threaten the territorial integrity of the country.

### Colonial Rule—A Balance Sheet

The contribution of British colonial rule to the improvement of social services was undoubtedly a significant step in the development of the Nigerian economy. Improvements in sanitation, the erection of modern hospitals, the training of health personnel at all levels, and research into tropical diseases led to a decline in the mortality rate and a rise in population. It might be argued that this policy was not entirely altruistic since the colonial regime was not unaware that a healthy and growing population would generate an increasing production of export commodities to meet imperial needs. Nevertheless, Nigeria, because of its size, needed population growth if it was to exploit effectively its natural resources and to create an adequate market for its domestic products.

Equally important was the introduction of western education by missionary societies with the encouragement of the colonial administration. Of course, the value of western education had been appreciated in the pre-colonial period by local rulers who sometimes sent their children to schools in England or welcomed missionaries largely because of the education that accompanied their task of evangelization. No doubt, with the passage of time and in the absence of colonial rule, western education would have spread from the coast and banks of the Niger into the hinterland. Colonialism, however, quickened the process, especially in the non-Muslim territories of the South where the missionaries, induced by the enthusiastic response of the inhabitants, sponsored the rapid spread of educational institutions.[4] The orientation of these institutions was toward the needs of the missionaries, administrators and foreign mercantile houses rather than the development of the colony. The primary schools and the few secondary institutions produced converts who could read the Bible and serve as junior cadres within the colonial administration and alien companies, enabling the expatriates to perform executive and managerial functions. Although a few Nigerians pursued higher education in England or in colleges at Yaba, Achimota and Fourah Bay, most were still relegated to subordinate positions. Given a situation in which for decades decision-making was the prerogative of the British administrator, a dependency mentality grew whereby the initiative for change was expected to come from the outside. To the extent that development is assumed to be "mainly an attitudinal problem," and a "mentality that expects others, rather than Africans, themselves, to take the initiative to mobilize the investments and, to make the effort toward African prosperity,"[5] the colonial educational system contributed to underdevelopment.

But there was another deleterious effect of the educational system. The emphasis of the curricula was on the humanities and on the economic and social situation in Europe; and this made it extremely difficult for the real developmental needs of the colony to be realized and attacked by graduates of the school system. The antiquated educational system has continued to serve as a norm until recent times.

One of the most important contributions that colonialism is said to have made to Nigeria's development was the modern system of communications which facilitated commercial intercourse. Prior to the advent of colonial rule the Rivers Niger and Benue had served as the main arteries of trade which linked both north and south. It had also been possible for traders to follow well-established bush-tracks over long distances. But these routes were subject to unpredictable interruptions as a result of local wars, and, in any event, the volume of commerce that they could support was limited, especially in the forest belt where the tse-tse fly limited the use of beasts of burden. The western and eastern railway lines built by the British to run from Lagos and Port Harcourt respectively to the North, supplemented by motorable roads and bridges, provided a safe, speedy and convenient bulk-carrier of goods. These transport facilities stimulated increased local production and, consequently, the growth of the colonial economy. The Railway and Marine Departments also improved the level of technology by training Nigerians in the skills associated with their operations.

However, the foregoing were indirect benefits from a colonial policy which saw the construction of railways and roads partly as a means of enforcing authority and partly as an avenue of exporting the primary produce increasingly needed by metropolitan industries. The alignment of the railway from the southern ports to the northern hinterland underlined their significance in the export trade rather than in enhancing the exchange of local goods and services.[6] The railway, of course, created new growth poles along its routes, but it also contributed to the decline of many pre-existing ones which lay outside its orbit. By and large, the railways really failed to integrate the economy of Nigeria more than had previously existed.

The colonial economy was geared toward meeting the external demand for such raw materials as could be produced locally. In parts of Eastern and Southern Africa where climatic factors were favourable to European settlement, land had been appropriated from the indigenous population and reserved for Europeans who came to dominate the export sector of the economy while the Africans were reduced to the role of hired labourers. This created the classical dual economy in which the indigenous sector remained stagnant while that of the alien enclave continued to expand and to derive increasing benefits.

In Nigeria, as in many other parts of West Africa, the European settler was kept at bay by a hostile climate, leaving the exploitation of the natural resources largely in the hands of the indigenous population. Nevertheless, while individual Nigerians were able to improve their standard of living, the economy still remained almost as underdeveloped as in the settler colonies. The first reason was the dependence of both economies on an export sector dominated by agriculture and/or mining. Naturally, because of her size and geographical location, Nigeria was able to avoid the plight of other colonial territories which were obliged to rely on a single crop economy for foreign exchange earnings. Palm produce from the east, cocoa from the west, cotton and groundnuts from the north were supplemented by rubber, timber, and tin to ensure a diversified economy that could weather the uncertainties of individual commodity prices in the international market. It has to be emphasized, however, that the Nigerians did suffer with all primary producers from the steady decline in the price of their crops.

As far as Nigeria was concerned, it was in the interest of the colonial rulers to promote the exploitation of raw materials required by the home-based industries. That accounted, at least in part, for the research activities of the Department of Agriculture which undertook studies on the cocoa and palm trees as well as the Forestry Department which explored for exportable produce.[7] Some benefits did accrue to the local economy by the concentrated application of modern scientific methods to the development of the natural resources. Apart from the phenomenal growth in the quantity and quality of the main export corps, a substantial number of valuable commodities were introduced into the Nigerian export market. These included rubber, ginger, citrus fruits, tobacco, ginger and cassava starch which were produced under the encouragement of the Department of Agriculture. The Department of Forestry, in addition to introducing Nigerian timber into the world market, promoted the exploitation and commercialization of gum arabic, raffia fibers, beeswax, and shea-nuts.

It has sometimes been argued that because colonized people were obliged to concentrate on growing cash crops for export, food crops were neglected and it became necessary for them to rely on food imports. In other words, the growth of cash crops distorted the existing economic system which had enabled the producer to balance the production of food and export crops. In colonial Nigeria, however, there does not seem to have been much deliberate shift from self-sufficiency in food production to dependence on food imports as a result of pressure to increase cash crops. Where importation of food into a particular region became necessary, this was the result of the specialization of economic functions, urbanization, and rising income of the population or unique local circumstances. Thus in his study of the palm oil economy Usoro has noted that the area where the palm trees flourished was characterized by poor soils which had traditionally precluded the inhabitants from attaining self-sufficiency in food production and obliged them to exchange palm oil with neighbours for other necessities.[8] Furthermore, in the cocoa and groundnut producing areas the small farmers did not entirely abandon the cultivation of food crops. They seem to have not only planted food crops but also supplemented their stocks with purchases where market forces made it necessary. Ultimately, only the new urban centres that were established under colonial rule required food imports and their needs were adequately met by the surrounding rural communities. Indeed, the production of food in Nigeria was so sufficient that some could have been exported to other colonies such as the Gold Coast (Ghana)— a development which occurred during World War II—if officials had not been preoccupied with the European market.

Nigeria was able to expand export production and maintain self-sufficiency in food probably because it represented the example of the vent-for-surplus theory propounded by Hla Myint, a development model which some scholars have found appropriate to Nigeria.[9] According to this theory Nigerian producers were induced by attractive exchange earnings to channel more land and labour, hitherto idle, into production for export. Hence, it was possible to expand rapidly the quantity of produce available from the country without either a change of technology or the sacrifice of traditional farming systems. Helleiner goes on to suggest that "since production functions were left largely untouched, he (the foreigner) cannot be accused of introducing an export bias to the economy."[10] This export bias, involving raw produce, is generally recognized as a significant index of underdevelopment. The argument could also be extended to include the fact that exports, first of slaves and then of palm produce, had formed part of the international exchange between the area which became Nigeria and Western Europe in the pre-colonial period. An opposing argument, however, would be that suggested by Andre Gundar Frank and elaborated by several others which, in point of fact, dates the process of underdevelopment to the sixteenth century and the beginning of the slave trade when parts of Africa were incorporated into the unfolding capitalist system.[11] Viewed from this perspective it becomes clear that the African economy had ceased to have an independent initiative long before the formal imposition of colonial rule. The only real difference was that, after the latter, African producers lost the flexibility of choosing their trading partners on the basis of market factors. Coupled with the fact that as primary producers they could not, (indeed, were not permitted) to compete from a position of economic strength, it becomes understandable how their underdevelopment was consolidated with the imposition of colonial rule.

While colonialism encouraged increased production of export crops, the establishment of industries was either neglected or forbidden until after World War II.[12] The reason, in part, was to avoid competition with the metropolitan industries which were supposed to have a reserved market in the colonies and to promote the profitable import trade and shipping interests of the foreign firms dominating the international trade of the colony. This failure to provide an industrial component to the Nigerian economy ensured that it could not escape from what has been called the "circle of poverty". Like other producers of raw materials, Nigeria's terms of trade in relation to the industrialized countries remained unfavourable. Hopkins has noted that after 1930 "a given 'basket' of exports purchased a progressively smaller 'basket' of imports and Africans had to step up the volume, and hence raise the value of cash crop production merely to maintain existing levels of import consumption."[13] Although there was some improvement in the net barter of trade for Nigeria at mid-century the terms of trade still favoured the industrialized countries, depriving the colony of capital essential for development.

Some efforts were made after World War II to establish a few processing plants but they were not the basic industries with backward and forward linkages which could sustain long-term development. Such industries as the manufacture of soap and cigarettes as well as the bottling of soft drinks were indeed embarked upon by foreign firms not because they wished to improve the economy but in order to keep out foreign competitors while realizing maximum profits from their limited, low-risk investments.

The dominant role played by these foreign companies in the Nigerian economy deserves particular attention. The most outstanding was the United Africa Company (U.A.C.). By 1920 the Nigerian trade was controlled by the British firms of the Niger Company and the African and Eastern Trading Company (A. & E.T.C.). In that year the Lever Brothers bought the Niger Company and nine years later absorbed the A. & E.T.C., thus paving the way for the birth of the U.A.C. which became a branch of the multinational Lever Brothers and Unilever Ltd. The U.A.C. alone, on the eve of World War II, controlled about 41.3 percent of the total import and export trade of Nigeria and thus was in a position to influence the direction of the economy.[14]

The U.A.C. and other smaller companies were largely responsible for the growth in Nigerian exports and imports but their total impact was to retard economic development. This arose from a number of factors. Attachment to the metropole where their headquarters were based obliged them to repatriate from the colony profits, interests, surplus liquid assets and about a half of the European salaries all of which could otherwise have been reinvested in the colony. In addition, much of the company tax was paid to the treasury of the metropole. It is also evident that the investment pattern of the firms showed a reluctance to undertake long-term risks and hence made planning difficult. Beyond this, the companies embarked on oligopolistic and monopsonistic practices which kept indigenous entrepreneurs out of the lucrative foreign trade. What is more, through these practices, it was possible for the firms to keep the local prices of raw produce deliberately low and thus discouraged optimum production. Thus, for example, the U.A.C. after its formation had less volume of trade than when the A. & E.T.C. and the Niger Company were in competition. But its profits continued to soar.

Equally critical for the development of the colonial economy was the nature of the banking policy. Until 1911, Nigeria, like the other British West

African colonies, relied for its currency on the Bank of British West Africa headed by Alfred L. Jones who also controlled the shipping monopoly, Elder Dempster Lines. During the period, apart from giving up the profits for such Central Bank services as the company performed, the colony lost its foreign exchange earnings to Britain. The responsibility for issuing the colonial currency was taken over in 1912 by the West African Currency Board which, in addition, received the mandate for managing the colonial reserves and the investment of the sizeable profits derived from its monetary operations.

The Board was an improvement on its predecessor but still was no substitute for a Central Bank which a sovereign country would operate to protect its development. As J. Mars pointed out:

> The West African Currency Board is, in fact, not a money issuing bank with power to vary the amount of currency at will but merely a passive money changer which receives superior money, i.e. London Sterling, and gives in return token money... i.e. West African currency.[15]

This token money was covered 100 percent after 1926 with the pound sterling which the colony acquired through the sale of export produce in Britain. The operation had serious damaging effects on the Nigerian economy. Given the generally steady deterioration of the terms of trade of primary producers, it was inevitable that the price levels of cash crops would be depressed and Nigerian farmers had to produce more in order to sustain their consumption of imported manufactured goods. Hence, the amount of local currency available tended to stagnate and even to decline. At the same time, the peasants were discouraged from increasing production of goods for domestic consumption on account of the low prices caused by the decreased volume of currency in circulation. The solution to this deflationary tendency was a flexible exchange rate with the pound sterling but the Board remained wedded to a rigid exchange policy from which only the metropole could benefit. Thus the pound sterling cover for the local currency maintained by the Board with the Bank of England provided the latter with a permanent loan which became available to the British capital market rather than to Nigeria. Had some of the money gained by the Board been loaned to Nigeria for development projects, considerable savings would have been obtained. As it transpired, Nigeria was obliged to resort to the open London money market, paying not only high interest rates but also the substantial costs involved in raising the loan. Hence, instead of aiding local development, the activities of the Board generally stultified it.

Within Nigeria commercial banking was dominated by the British companies, Barclays Bank and the Bank of British West Africa. Most of the criticisms levied above against foreign firms apply with equal force to these banks. In addition, it was their operation that promoted the import-export trade, the dependent sector of the economy, between Nigeria and the metropole. Because of their limited and conservative perception of banking functions the banks contributed little to the economic development of the colony. In particular, they failed to expand sufficiently to assist in mobilizing indigenous assets which could have been ploughed into productive channels. Next, by maintaining large liquid and external balances, they deprived the economy of funds which could have been utilized for development. Finally, they proved reluctant to advance loans to indigenous entrepreneurs, preferring instead Europeans and Levantines who made and repatriated enormous profits.

## Post World War II Development Strategies

Even before the Second World War ended Britain had recognized that the high noon of colonial exploitation had passed in Nigeria, as elsewhere, and that the formulation of a development strategy was necessary. Following the enactment of the Colonial Development and Welfare Act, which required each colony to draw up a development plan, British officials in Nigeria prepared "A Ten-Year Plan of Development and Welfare." The plan envisaged an expenditure of £ 55,000,000 over a ten-year period with £ 23,000,000 to be contributed by the British government through the Colonial Development and Welfare Fund created by the Act. Nigeria was to provide the rest. The emphasis of the Plan was on the improvement of social services and public utilities such as health, education, electricity and water supplies as well as the construction of roads and telecommunication networks. The Plan was revised in 1956, at the expiration of the ten years, with transportation absorbing about forty percent of the capital expenditure.

Most of the equipment and personnel required for implementing these plans were supplied from Britain so that a sizeable proportion of the expenditure was re-cycled into the British economy. More pertinent, however, is the criticism levied in 1946 and subsequently that the programmes did not address the issue of large-scale industrialization which was critical for meaningful development. Furthermore, the Plans continued to emphasize not really the improvement of agriculture, which was necessary to feed the growing population, but the increased production of export crops for which Nigeria was already famous in the world market.[16]

Although the Nigerian farmers responded to the demand for greater quantities of export crops, the returns on their labour stagnated, a factor which continued to hinder optimum output. The reason for this trend was the introduction of the Marketing Boards, born of the West African Cocoa Produce Board (renamed West African Produce Control Board in 1942) which had been established as a wartime measure in 1939. Through the earlier Board, the British government had purchased export crops from Nigerian farmers generally at low prices and then resold them at considerable profit (except in 1939 and 1941) in the U.S. and U.K. markets. The profit, amounting for cocoa alone to over £ 9,000,000 sterling became "a forced loan to the British government—a loan subsequently to be repaid in much depreciated currency and without interest."[17]

The succeeding Boards continued the practice of paying the Nigerian producers prices deliberately set below world prices, retaining the difference ostensibly to supplement local prices should the world prices fall. The supplementation never occurred. The policy of price stabilization in fact became a ruse to accumulate large sterling balances in the metropole. Thus by 1954 almost £ 120 million had been raised and invested in United Kingdom securities. But in that year the World Bank recommended that this amount and subsequent additions be employed for development in Nigeria. Ultimately, the Marketing Board assets contributed little to development, much of it being frittered away in enterprises of dubious value by the emerging national bourgeoisie.[18] Undoubtedly the Marketing Board policy helped in mobilizing reserves for development, even if that had not been its original objective. It must not be forgotten, however, that the allocation of those reserves to projects which largely enhanced the attractiveness of the urban environment—an allocation that discriminated against the rural areas—ultimately contributed to the decline in agricultural production.

## Concluding Remarks

The balance sheet of colonialism in Nigeria, then, is not easy to draw up for it depends on the theoretical and hence the ideological orientation of the individual. Optimistic capitalists or liberals who favour the idea of progress and such theories as Rostow's "stages of growth" would inevitably conclude that on balance colonialism, by creating Nigeria, introducing its citizens to modern technology, improving agriculture, social welfare, public utilities and the communication network as well as laying the foundations for a modern system of government contributed to growth and development. Colonialism, then, was a necessary and logical experience which galvanized the backward Nigerians into a modern era, preparing their country and their minds for entry into self-sustained economic development.

For Marxist and radical scholars who share a different perspective of the development process, the advantages which colonialism is said to have conferred pale when compared to the enforced, and apparently permanent dependence of the Nigerian economy on external factors beyond its control. It is not without interest and significance that the prospects of Nigeria's development have considerably brightened since her membership of the Oil Producing and Exporting Countries (OPEC) which has broken the price control hitherto imposed by the developed countries and enabled her to realize optimum income from one natural resource. This income is now being ploughed into the industrial and agricultural sectors and generally has facilitated the take-over of the commanding heights of the economy by the indigenous population.

### BIBLIOGRAPHY

BERRY, SARA. *Cocoa, Custom, and Socio-Economic Change in Rural Western Nigeria.* Oxford, 1975.
CARNEY, DAVID. "Requirements for African Economic Development." In *Africa in the Seventies and Eighties: Issues in Development.* Edited by Frederick S. Arkhurst. New York, 1970, pp. 176-195.

HAGENDORN, J. S. "The Origins of the Groundnut Trade in Northern Nigeria." Ph. D. thesis, University of London, 1966.

HARRIS, RICHARD, ed. *The Political Economy of Africa.* Cambridge, Mass., 1975.

HAWKINS, E. K. *Road Transport in Nigeria.* London, 1958.

HELLEINER, G. K. *Peasant Agriculture, Government, and Economic Growth in Nigeria.* Homewood, 1966.

HOPKINS, A. G. *An Economic History of West Africa.* New York, 1973.

LAGOS, GUSTAVO. *International Stratification and Underdeveloped Countries.* Chapel Hill, 1963.

MARTIN, A. *The Oil Palm Economy of the Ibibio Farmer.* Ibadan, 1956.

MARX, KARL. *Capital,* vol. I. Translated by Samuel Moore and Edward Aveling. Budapest, 1976.

MUNRO, J. FORBES. *Africa and the International Economy, 1800-1960.* London, 1976.

MYINT, HLA. "The 'Classical Theory' of International Trade and the Underdeveloped Countries." *Economic Journal* LXVIII (20):317-337.

Nigeria, Federal Ministry of Economic Development. *National Development Plan, 1962-68.* Lagos, 1962.

NIXON, CHARLES R. "The Role of the Marketing Boards in the Political Evolution of Nigeria." In *Growth and Development of the Nigerian Economy.* Edited by Carl K. Eicher and Carl Liedholm. Michigan State University, 1970, pp. 156-162.

NKRUMAH, KWAME. *Neo-Colonialism, the Last Stage of Imperialism.* New York, 1965.

PERHAM, MARGERY, ed. *Mining, Commerce, and Finance in Nigeria.* London, 1948.

——. *The Native Economies of Nigeria.* London, 1946.

ROSTOW, W. W. *The Stages of Economic Growth: a Non-Communist Manifesto.* Cambridge, 1960.

SZENTES, TAMAS. *The Political Economy of Underdevelopment.* Budapest, 1976.

USORO, ENO J. *The Nigerian Oil Palm Industry.* Ibadan, 1974.

WORSLEY, PETER. *The Third World.* London, 1964.

## NOTES

1 The classic exposition of this view which others have modified is W. W. Rostow, *The Stages of Economic Growth: A Non-Communist Manifesto* (Cambridge, 1960).

2 Karl Marx, *Capital,* vol. I, trans. by Samuel Moore and Edward Aveling (New York, 1967), p. 451. (Cf. Tamas Szentes, *The Political Economy of Underdevelopment* (Budapest, 1976), p. 136.

3 Peter Worsley, *The Third World* (London, 1964), pp. 14-15 and 50-51; Gustavo Lagos, *International Stratification and Underdeveloped Countries* (Chapel Hill, 1963), p. 6.

4 Political consideration led the British administrators to keep missionary education out of the Muslim north.

5 David Carney, "Requirements for African Economic Development," in Frederick S. Arkhurt (ed.), *Africa in the Seventies and Eighties: Issues in Development* (New York, 1970), pp. 176-195.

6 E. K. Hawkins, *Road Transport in Nigeria* (London, 1958), pp. 22-23.

7 For a valuable discussion of these developments see Margery Perham (ed.), *The Native Economies of Nigera* (London, 1946), pp. 217-291 and Margery Perham (ed.), *Mining, Commerce, and Finance in Nigeria* (London, 1948), pp. 137-175.

8 Eno J. Usoro, *The Nigerian Oil Palm Industry* (Ibadan, 1974), pp. 58-59. See also A. Martin, *The Oil Palm Economy of the Ibibio Farmer* (Ibadan, 1956), p. 19.

9 Hla Myint, "The 'Classical Theory' of International Trade and the Under-Developed Countries," *Economic Journal,* vol. LXVIII, 20, pp. 317-337; G. K. Helleiner, *Peasant Agriculture, Government, and Economic Growth in Nigeria* (Homewood, 1966); Sara Berry, *Cocoa, Custom, and Socio-Economic Change in Rural Western Nigeria* (Oxford, 1975); and J. S. Hagendorn, "The Origins of the Groundnut Trade in Northern Nigeria," Ph. D. Thesis, University of London, 1966.

10 Helleiner, p. 12.

11   Richard Harris (ed.), *The Political Economy of Africa* (Cambridge, Mass., 1975), p. 10; J. Forbes Munro, *Africa and the International Economy,* 1800-1960 (London, 1976), p. 14.

12   A most useful source of information on these foreign companies as well as a valuable critique of their activities will be found in chapters by J. Mars in Perham, *Mining, Commerce and Finance.*

13   A. G. Hopkins, *An Economic History of West Africa* (New York), p. 254. See also Helleiner, pp. 18-31. Nkrumah commented in 1965 that although Ghana and Nigeria have trebled cocoa production their gross earnings have declined from £ 125 million to £ 117 million. Kwame Nkrumah, *Neo-Colonialism, the Last Stage of Imperialism* (New York, 1965), p. 10.

14   See Mars in Perham, *Mining, Commerce and Finance.*

15   Ibid., p. 186.

16   Federal Ministry of Economic Development, *National Development Plan, 1962-68* (Lagos, 1962), p. 6.

17   Helleiner, p. 156.

18   Charles R. Nixon, "The Role of the Marketing Boards in the Political Evolution of Nigeria," in Carl K. Eicher and Carl Leidholm (eds.), *Growth and Development of the Nigerian Economy* (Michigan State University, 1970), pp. 156-162.

# Economic Dependence:
# The Problem of Definition

OLAYINKA SONAIKE and BODE OLOWOPOROKU

*University of Ife, Ile-Ife, Nigeria*

"ECONOMIC DEPENDENCE" IS A TERM that is widely used to portray the relationship of inequality between the underdeveloped countries and the advanced, prosperous countries on which the former depend for technical and industrial know-how. It is essentially a structural concept that embodies other ideas and values, most of them negative in their connotations. Most of the time, the phenomenon subsumed by the term is assumed usage, and attempt is seldom made to define it. Yet the phenomenon must be adequately defined if it is to be properly understood.

The definition of "economic dependence" is problematic, primarily because in order for a definition to be useful it must meet the test of adequacy and unambiguity. As used in contemporary development literature, "economic dependence" captures the significant structural relationships among many economies and nation states with varying degrees of economic, political and military power; but the effects of their interaction are constantly changing, intertemporally and spatially. To come up with an adequate and useful definition which covers existing conditions and illuminates their interaction and dynamics is a challenging task indeed.

In this paper, our approach to the problem of defining "economic dependence" will be historical. The emphasis is on two schools of thought: the traditional or orthodox school and the radical or progressive school. By discussing these two schools we will become increasingly aware of the problems associated with any definition. We will show that none of the two schools has provided an enduring definition precisely because of the problems associated with the phenomenon. We will indicate that a dynamic definition promises to be more durable.

### The Traditional School and the Definitions of Economic Dependence

The Great Depression of the 1920s to early 1930s gave birth to the possibilities of economic dependence. Before that period, neoclassical economic theory predicted harmony among all components of the world economy. In this theory trade was regarded as the catalyst which would bring economic interdependence, share benefits fairly, and spread development to all nations of the world irrespective of their size and structure of production.

However, this myth of international harmony was called to question during the Depression of the 1920s to 1930s. While Keynesian economics attacked the golden concept of accumulation in the neoclassical, metaphysical apparatus, the "traditional school of dependence" attacked the neoclassical international division of labour based on comparative advantage.[1] This school was led by Prebisch[2] and Lewis.[3] Prebisch argued against the continued reliance of Latin American countries on exports of primary commodities to provide the dynamic for growth and made a case for industrialization as the most attractive alternative. Prebisch argued that:

> In Latin America, reality is undermining the outdated scheme of the international division of labour which achieved great importance in the 19th century and as a theoretical concept, continued to exert considerable influence until very recently. Under that scheme, the specific task that fell to Latin America as part of the periphery of the world economic system was that of producing food and raw materials for the great industrial centres.[4]

Lewis shared Prebisch's opinion that concentration on primary production made the Caribbean and Latin American countries dependent. Furthermore, he was much concerned with how the old international division of labour has created surplus labour or unemployment in the dependent countries. An advocate of labour intensive types of industrialization, Lewis formulated his popular model of "Development with unlimited supply of labour" in response to problems faced by dependent economies.[5]

The traditional school of economic thought defined "economic dependence" in terms of critical dependence on primary exports which constituted the major activities of the developing countries. In order to liquidate their economic dependence, the recommended solution was industrialization, and it was the labour intensive type of industrialization that was recommended—a strategy that gave birth to the import substitution pattern of industrialization that is now widespead. In the words of Hoffman, "...the structure of the manufacturing sector of the economy has always followed a uniform pattern. The food, textile, leather and furniture industries—which we define as consumer goods industries—always develop first during the process of industrialisation".[6]

However, neither external dependence nor dependence on primary exports has in reality been reduced. Initial industrialization failed because of rising import demand and failure of traditional exports. This was followed by a new drive to increase exports of primary produce, and in many cases this was pressed so hard as to constrain the growth of other parts of the economy by starving them of production factors. There was a further drive to mechanise the primary exports which aggravated economic dependence through the need for imported materials and exports outlets.[7]

Disenchantment with the old definitions of dependence in the face of growing unequal relationships continued. The search for a new definition was found in the structuralist school, in itself a variant of the traditional school of dependence. The main thesis of this group is that independent industrialization could only be successfully accomplished within large states, a thesis that found empirical support in the fact that import substitution industrialization progressed faster and more easily within large Latin American countries such as Brazil and Argentina than in smaller states. Like the classical school of thought which preceded it, the structuralist argument is that industrialization and specialization are limited by the size of the market; and therefore structural dependence is a function of size and structure of the economy. The paradox is that the economic limitations imposed by the size of the market cannot be made up by increasing preferential treatment and aid from the advanced countries. Indeed, the effect of preferential treatment, aid and protectionism is to create high-cost industries which would not be able to stand international competition eventually. Small countries which establish small sized industries under protectionism create another form of dependence known as functional dependence. This theme may be expressed as follows:

> The question of economic dependence is not all unrelated to that of size of countries. In its attempt to overcome dependence by increasing and diversifying production and reducing its reliance on foreign suppliers for the bulk of the goods and services which it requires, a small country suffers from the basic constraints of a narrow range of natural resources and inadequate size stemming from small population...It is partially in this context that economic integration becomes important.[8]

For this reason, it was argued, the best way of getting out of dependence was by regional integration. This was what gave impetus to Latin American integration of which LAFTA was the first expression.[9]

The major contention of the traditional school on dependence is that internal structural factors determine the type and degree of dependence. Therefore, for economic dependence to be eliminated, there must be changes in internal structures. Rarely is economic dependence seen as being externally generated and determined. The weakness in the theory of the traditional school is that attempts to implement their prescriptions have actually aggravated and increased economic dependence. Since the prescriptions of this school have not succeeded in eliminating economic dependence, a radical school of thought has emerged to offer a new radical, alternative perspective. It is their definition of economic dependence that we will now examine.

## The Progressive or Radical School: Their Approach to Dependency

The progressive school analyses economic dependence from the historical, dialectical viewpoint. Economic dependence is examined through the perspective of external economic relations and is defined in terms of the historical relationship between a dependent and a dominant nation. The main agent in a dependence-dominance relationship is capitalism. As Frank phrases it, "Historical research demonstrates that contemporary underdevelopment is in large part the historical product of past and continuing economic and other relations between the satellite (dependent) and the new developed (metropolitan dominant) countries. Furthermore, these relations are an essential part of the structure and development of the capitalist system on a world scale as a whole."[10]

Although most of the progressive writers on economic dependence do not agree on all points, they tend to emphasize the following hypotheses with remarkable frequency:[11]

(a) economic dependence is a result of world expansion of capitalism
(b) dependence leads to economic exploitation and repatriation of economic surplus (i.e., sucking of capital out of the dependent countries to the dominant countries)
(c) economic dependence leads to underdevelopment.

In the view of the progressive school, country $B$ is dependent on country $A$ and country $A$ is dominant over country $B$ if major economic (political) decisions, conditions or policies in country $B$ are or can be *critically* affected, determined or influenced by decisions and policies of country $A$. At the same time, the converse does not hold, i.e., similar economic activities in country $A$ cannot be affected or influenced by the decisions and policies taken by country $B$.[12] With this standard definition of economic dependence, we can proceed to define economic interdependence and economic autarky. Economic interdependence is a situation where the policies and decisions made in any one country can affect the situation in the other countries with which it maintains economic relations. Economic autarky is when the decision of $A$ does not affect $B$ at all and that of $B$ does not affect $A$ at all.

The progressive school has isolated many forms of economic dependence.[13] There is trade dependence in which economic changes in the dependent economy are completely determined by changes in imports and exports. Imports provide the major part of available manufactured goods either in the form of finished goods or in the form of components to be assembled locally behind tariff walls; often it is both. They also provide the capital and intermediate goods on which limited domestic, industrialization can take place. As a result the level of resource utilization in manufacturing is determined externally. Also social cohesion and political stability are affected by the level of imported inflation. The level of export is the major determinant of the capacity to import both capital and consumer goods via foreign exchange earnings. Where the external terms of trade cannot be improved by the dependent economy, as is usually the case, the phenomenon of export dependence may be detrimental to a country's development prospects. Export concentration, both by market and commodity, may also be detrimental. Although attempts have been made to refute this, such efforts have not been totally persuasive.[14] The evidence shows that export capacity affects the volume and distribution of National Income and the domestic standard of living, particularly where a large section of the population is dependent on export earnings as is the case in developing countries where farmers constitute the major export forces.

There is also technological dependence in which domestic technology is dependent on imported technology for its transformation. As a result domestic factor proportions and relative income distribution are determined by foreign considerations. In addition, the rate of domestic technological transformation is determined by foreign corporate policies on research and development expenditure, staff deployment, patents, licenses, etc. Thus the domestic economy is usually dragged along a technological growth path which it probably would not have chosen if it had a choice.

The ownership of productive resources is another factor in dependence. In many countries, foreigners own a substantial proportion of capital investment in the dependent economy. Because the control of natural resources and the ownership of capital are foreign, dividend, technology, growth and employment policies are externally determined and dictated; so also are product type and quality policies. These factors which determine the long-term prospects of any economy, combined with the repatriation of profits, make some underdeveloped economies net exporters of capital despite their capital shortage.[15]

These are the major features of economic dependence. Their effects are fairly obvious. First, the national authority of a dependent economy is unable to control, plan, manage and direct the economy along desired paths. Their manipulation of economic variables like wages, taxes, interest rates, etc. may not produce expected results because many of the variables do not possess postulated relationships with one another because they are externally determined. The second reason flows from the first, and it is that economic development becomes a chance happening, completely dependent on external factors. Government desires for the elimination of poverty, regional disparities in industrial distribution, and for diversification of economic activities cannot be realized. The dependent economy is condemned to stagnation and underdevelopment for as long as external exploitative relationships are maintained.

The problem with the definition of economic dependence proposed by the progressive school is that it attempts too much. It ties the creation of empires and spheres of economic influence and control with a desire to export surplus capital, maintain desired domestic rates of profit and dominate the world market by monopolistic operations. The theory is a partial one in that it emphasizes primarily the domestic, economic, political and social institutions in the advanced capitalist countries with inadequate attention to corresponding institutions in the dependent economies. Economic dependence depicts a type of relationship among economies and nation states. If there are immanent laws of capitalism which created imperialism, we should look for features within the underdeveloped countries which forced them into subordinate roles in the international division of labour that emerged at the point of their contact with capitalist countries. From the point of view of the dependent economies, these are the relevant factors to look for if we are ever going to develop a strategy for the elimination of dependence.

History shows that it was not only technological superiority that enhanced the subjugation and domination of the underdeveloped countries at the point of contact: cunning, widespread violence, trade, and other factors played various roles.[16] There is, however, no denying the influence of technological superiority, particularly the existence of the gun, in softening up various societies for European control and dehumanization. It is now a matter of history that societies which emerged as underdeveloped countries were politically and militarily weak at the period when they were incorporated into the world capitalist system. Any attempt to examine this thesis further will take us farther afield, off course, into the explanations for differences in rates of development among nations. We do not intend to do this. However, the other set of factors which maintain economic dependence are more relevant to us here because of the implication that they probably will be removable, thus providing an escape route from economic dependence. The single most important factor in this respect is the political and social power structure within the dependent economies themselves.[17] Two classes of people can be recognized within the dependent economy—the centre comprising the capitalists, the political bureaucrats and the landed aristocrats, and the periphery comprising workers and the peasants who have been marginalized by the capitalist system.[18] The centre is usually in harmony with the advanced capitalist countries while the periphery is not.

The identification of the well-being of the centre, whose members are usually the dominant power group with foreign interests, perpetuates economic dependence. We can break down the centre into senior civil servants, cash crop farmers, businessmen in commerce (the manufacturers' representatives) and pseudo manufacturers whose semi-finished products are imported. In the periphery class we have food crop farmers and small scale businessmen. In practice, the farmer groups may not be quite distinct. Although we cannot completely identify the cash crop farmers with the business elite in their foreign purpose, it is still true that their interests are linked with external business interests by unconscious choice.

Since the economic activities of the centre of the periphery are tightly linked with foreign business interests, any domestic policy that creates economic independence is resisted, usually by such economic arguments as reduction in efficiency, slow rate of progress, and misallocation of resources. Correspondingly, the belief in the open economy approach to development and the efficacy of the "law of comparative advantage" is strong. The centre of the periphery lacks the capacity to transform the dependent economy structurally.[19] Part of the reason is that the incumbents of political roles are usually recruited from the elite whose economic and cultural orientations are outward-looking and their strategy for economic development always calls for inducements for foreign investment, more external aid, and the expansion of the primary export sector. Each of these measures tightens the screws of economic dependence on the advanced capitalist countries.

The progressive theories have their limitations. By concentrating on two-actor relationships—the Metropolis-Periphery—they have neglected the dynamic changes in the system. The historic relationship forged between the advanced capitalist countries and the underdeveloped areas has been transformed to include several intermediate economic and military powers. The socialist block countries have also entered the system, armed with considerable technological power and political ambition and ability to affect the existing two-actor relationship.

To recapitulate, the orthodox school could not provide an adequate definition of economic dependency because it identified the wrong causes and postulated the wrong nature of the phenomenon; and the progressive school has also misperceived and neglected some relatively new and emerging elements in the phenomenon, thus leaving us with the task of coming up with a new definition of economic dependence.

## Towards a New Definition of Economic Dependency

The dynamic nature of the development process implies that no one definition of economic dependence will have continuous intertemporal and interspace validity. This is one of the major problems of definition. The nature and degree of dependence and the participants in the phenomenon keep changing. As they change, new definitions will be required.

We have identified the main causes of economic dependence as the exploitation of a dependent economy by capitalist economies, the lack of indigenous technological knowledge, and the existence of a political, social and economic power structure favourable to the perpetuation of dependency. *The fact that a developed nation depends on foreign trade to raise or maintain its living standards would not make it economically dependent provided it possesses a competitive technology and is not politically dominated by outsiders.* Of course it can be argued that no economy is completely independent since all economies are inter-related. This generalization befogs the fact of unequal exchange between the developed capitalist nations and underdeveloped areas.

Economic dependence has evolved from the two-actor situation to the multi-actor situation. The factors in this transformation include the so-called middle economic and military powers: the emergence of OPEC nations, some of them rich in oil resources and little else, the socialist countries, and the new forms and institutions of economic integration among groups of capitalist, socialist and Third World countries. It is an interesting question to speculate about what new economic relationships will be forged from the interaction of these new forces.

In trying to answer this question, we make the following observations. First, all nations—capitalist, socialist and underdeveloped—now subscribe to the political imperative of a fairer, international economic order. Whether this implies the elimination of exploitation of dependent economies by the developed capitalist world is not yet obvious; and some doubt if it is a genuine effort given the failure of several international conferences, meetings and symposia on the matter.

Secondly, the continued growth of the advanced capitalist economies and their high standard of living are tied to their continued exploitation of the underdeveloped countries which supply their raw materials and purchase their finished products at prices dictated by the capitalist countries. An improvement in the standard of living of the underdeveloped countries, through increased domestic manufacturing, for instance, may mean a drastic reduction in the standard of living of the advanced countries, possibly leading to social and political instability. The oil crisis of 1973 provides a case study.

Thirdly, the effects of economic integration, in both developed and developing economies, on economic relationships among nations are not easy to capture. The process of economic integration is continuing on all fronts. The European captialist countries appreciate the advantages of the EEC and are expanding its membership and objectives; the Socialist states are also strengthening their co-operation; and the underdeveloped countries—differentiated by ideology, limited by their poor technology, possessing similar, underdeveloped resources, and often lacking considerable social cohesion and the political will to fight the challenge posed by the two other "Worlds" struggling for their allegiance—are still trying to define the terms which will build lasting economic groupings among them.[20]

Given this background, we postulate a future world economy with three structural configurations: the super-dominant economies of the advanced capitalist and socialist countries; the emerging sub-dominant economies which are likely to be recruited from the large and relatively more advanced capitalist-oriented countries of the underdeveloped nations such as Brazil, Argentina, India, Nigeria and Egypt, plus some "drop-outs" from the former club of the imperial system such as Portugal; and the perpetually aid-dependent economies, the so-called "poorest of the poor" nations. Two main forces could be acting on the "poorest of the poor" dependent economies. The first force comes from the super-dominant countries. Their control of the technological base of industrialization and development capital might lead to the location of intermediate industries in the sub-dominant economies which would make them regional export centres of industrial goods and services whose blueprints and profits are controlled by super-dominant economies. In this structure, the relationship between the sub-dominant countries and the super-dominant countries is direct while that between them and the "poorest of the poor" is indirect. Thus India could become the regional service centre for its area; Egypt for some Arab areas; Nigeria for the sub-region of West Africa; Zaire for Central Africa; and Brazil and Argentina for Latin American areas. The super-dominant nations would prefer this arrangement to direct exploitation which would inevitably provoke a confrontation with many atomistic economies, either singly or in their loose economic groups.

Technological knowledge is the main instrument of control and the means of sucking economic surplus from the sub-dominant economies. Because of their relative scarcity, know-how and materials would tend to be highly overpriced. The rate of economic progress in the sub-dominant economies would be largely determined by events in the super-dominant economies for a long time. In turn, events in the sub-dominant economies would largely determine the rate of growth in more dependent economies.

For this development scenario to materialize, two factors are crucial: the continuing monopoly of technological knowledge by the super-dominant nations and the existence of favourable power and social groups attitudes in the sub-dominant and perpetually aid-dependent economies. However, the re-direction of the external orientation of the power groups which control sub-dominant systems and the development of appropriate technologies and knowledge functional within the society might provide an escape route from economic dependency.

The second force comes from the Socialist states, either individually or as groups, as they attempt to find recruits for their ideological camp. Up to now, the aims of the Socialist international economic relations have been mainly political, to demonstrate the superiority of socialism to capitalism. Some of the formerly underdeveloped economies which have taken off industrially give credit to the USSR for their economic achievements.[21]

It is postulated that when a nation is launching itself on an irreversible path of socialist development, genuine technological aid to enable it to stand on its feet may start pouring in. The relationship is devoid of economic ex-ploitative motive since productive resources are not owned by foreigners and surplus value is not appropriated for repatriation. The relationship between the USSR and China during and immediately after the Chinese revolution and the relationship between Russia and Cuba up till now are examples of this socialist approach. The rapid transformation in Cuba resulting from the rela-tionship has been well documented.[22]

The evidence seems to suggest that while the relationship between poor, dependent states and the super-dominant states reinforces economic dependence, stagnation and poverty, their relationship with socialist states provides an escape route. The only path to economic independence for underdeveloped countries, which has any historical precedent, is the cutting of links with monopoly capital and undergoing a socialist revolution.[23] It could be argued that the subsidiaries of the Multinational Corporations which operate in the sub-dominant nations would not add to their dependence burden or ex-port dependence to underdeveloped countries serviced directly by sub-dominant economies. We are not persuaded by this argument. There are at least three reasons why the emergence of the sub-dominant nations is detrimental to the future of the underdeveloped countries and therefore merits the attention we have given it. First, there is a real possibility of increase in the rate of exploitation resulting from either increase in product prices or decrease in product prices which is more than compensated for by drastic fall in product quality. For example, while the prices of Volkswagen cars imported into Nigeria from Brazil are relatively lower than the German imports, the quality decline has been serious. Secondly, the use of the sub-dominant nations as 'en-trepots' for underdeveloped nations reduces the quality and quantity of the technological knowledge available to the latter and complicates the process of acquisition of technology by the most dependent nations. Also, the conditions of technological transfer from the super-dominant to the sub-dominant na-tions—and licensing agreements may be cited—tends to curtail the amount of technological knowledge available to the most dependent nations.

## Concluding Remarks

We have analysed the main problems relating to the definition of the phenomenon of economic dependence. Our thesis is that an adequate and useful definition of economic dependence must provide an insight into the causes, effects and nature of economic dependency as well as empirical evidence for it. For different reasons we took issue with the various definitions offered by both the orthodox and progressive schools of economic thought. Recognizing the emerging relationships among nations, we have expanded the two-actor framework in which the underdeveloped economy is subject to direct exploitation by and dependence on the capitalist states into a multiple-actor system in which socialist states become significant actors and underdeveloped countries are further stratified into sub-dominant and most dependent states.

Obviously, the ability of any one or a group of underdeveloped nations emancipating themselves from the dependence trap depends on their ability to identify the dominant factor responsible for their dependency and mobilise resources and political will to eliminate it. The main factors responsible have been identified as close ties with the capitalist world, disparities in technological knowledge, and weak political institutions. To eliminate dependency, it will be necessary that the periphery be in complete control of political power and its leaders be in a position to redirect their external orientation. This is unlikely to happen without a social revolution.

### BIBLIOGRAPHY

ALLENDE, S. "Speech to the United Nations." In *International Firms and Modern Imperialism,* edited by H. Radice. Penguin, 1975.

BARAN, PAUL A. *The Political Economy of Growth.* London: Modern Reader Paperbacks, 1958.

BROKKFILED, HAROLD. *Interdependent Development.* London: Methuen and Co., 1975.

BROWN, BARRAT. *The Economics of Imperialism.* Penguin, 1974.

CARDOSO, F. H. "Dependency and Development in Latin America." *New Left Review* 74 (July-August 1972).

DEMAS, WILLIAM G. *Essays on Caribbean Integration and Development.* Jamaica: Institute of Social and Economic Research, University of the West Indies, 1976.

FAGAN, R. R. "Cuban Revolutionary Politics." *Monthly Review* 23 (1972).

FRANK, A. G. *Capitalism and Underdevelopment in Latin America.* New York: Monthly Review Press, 1969.

———. "The Development of Underdevelopment." In *Imperialism and Underdevelopment: A Reader.* Edited by R. I. Rhodes. New York: Monthly Review Press, 1970.

GALTUNG, JOHAN. "A Structural Theory of Imperialism." *The African Review* 1 (1972-1973): 93-138.

HOPKINS, A. G. *An Economic History of West Africa.* London, 1973.

KARAM, A. E. "The Meaning of Dependence." *The Developing Economies* XIV: 3 (1976): 201-211.

LEWIS, W. A. "Economic Development with Unlimited Supplies of Labour." *The Manchester School* 22 (1954): 139-191.

———. "The Industrialization of the British West Indies." *Caribbean Economic Review,* May 1950.

MACBEAN, A. I. "The Short-term Consequences of Export Instability." In *Economic Policy for Development.* Edited by I. Livingstone. Penguin, 1977.

MAGDOFF, HARRY. "Imperialism Without Colonies." In *Studies in the Theory of Imperialism.* Edited by R. Owen and Bod Sutcliff. London: Longman, 1972.

OLOWOPOROKU, BODE. "ECOWAS: Some Unsettled Issues." *The Journal of Business and Social Studies.* New Series, 1978.

OLOWOPOROKU, BODE and SONAIKE, OLAYINKA. "A Critique of African Development Strategy with Reference to External Economic Relationship." *African Development Studies* 1 (1977): 84-105.

PINTO, A. and KNAKAL, J. "The Centre-Periphery System Twenty Years Later." *Social and Economic Studies* 22 (1973): 64-70.

PREBISCH, R. *The Economics of Development of Latin America and Its Problems.* New York: U.N. Department of Social and Economic Affairs, 1960.

RITLER, A. R. M. "Growth, Strategy and Economic Performance in Revolutionary Cuba: Past, Present and Prospective." *Social and Economic Studies* 21 (1972):313-337.

RODNEY, WALTER. *How Europe Underdeveloped Africa.* Dar-es-Salaam: Tanzania Publishing House, 1972.

SEARS, D., ed. *Cuba: The Economic and Social Revolution.* North Carolina University Press, 1964.

SONAIKE, OLAYINKA. "Human Needs, Economic Development and Economic Nationalism: The African Case." Mimeographed. University of Ife: Ile-Ife, 1978.

SUTCLIFF, R. B. *Industry and Underdevelopment.* London: Addison-Wesley, 1971.

SZENTES, TAMAS. *The Political Economy of Underdevelopment.* Budapest: Akademiaikiado, 1973.

## NOTES

1   Bode and Olayinka, "A Critique of African Development Strategy with Reference to External Economic Relationships", *African Development Studies*, 1977.
2   Prebisch, *The Economics of Development of Latin America and Its Problems*, New York, 1960.
3   Lewis, "The Industrialization of the British West Indies", *Caribbean Economic Review*, 1950; "Economic Development with Unlimited Supplies of Labour," *The Manchester School*, vol. 22, 1954, pp. 139-191.
4   Prebisch, op. cit. 1960, p. 1.
5   Lewis, op. cit. 1950; 1954.
6   Sutcliff, *Industry and Underdevelopment*, Addison-Wesley, London, 1971, p. 23.
7   Ritler, "Growth, Strategy and Economic Performance in Revolutionary Cuba: Past, Present and Prospective", *Social and Economic Studies*, Vol. 21, 1972.
8   Demas, *Essays on Caribbean Integration and Development*, University of West Indies, Jamaica, 1976.
9   Brokkfiled, *Interdependent Development*, Methuen and Co., 1975, pp. 129-50.
10  Frank, "The Development of Underdevelopment", in Rhodes (ed.), *Imperialism and Underdevelopment: A Reader*, Monthly Review Press, New York, 1970, p. 55.
11  Frank, *Capitalism and Underdevelopment in Latin America*, Monthly Review Press, New York, 1969.
12  Karam, "The Meaning of Dependence", *The Developing Economies*, Vol. XIV, No. 3, 1976, pp. 201-11.
13  Szentes, *The Political Economy of Underdevelopment*, Budapest, 1973.
14  Macbean, "The Short-term Consequences of Export Instability", in Livingstone (ed.), *Economic Policy for Development*, Penguin, 1977.
15  Allende, "Speech to the United Nations", In Radice (ed.), *International Firms and Modern Imperialism*, Penguin, 1975; Brown, *The Economics of Imperialism*, Penguin, 1974; Cardoso, "Dependency and Development in Latin America", *New Left Review*, No. 74, 1972; Magdoff, "Imperialism Without Colonies", In Owen and Sutcliff (cds.), *Studies in the Theory of Imperialism*, Longman, London, 1972.
16  Hopkins, *An Economic History of West Africa*, London, 1973; Rodney, *How Europe Underdeveloped Africa*, Tanzania Publishing House, Dar-es-Salaam, 1972.
17  Magdoff, op. cit. 1972.
18  Galtung, "A Structural Theory of Imperialism", *The African Review*, Vol. I, 1972/73, pp. 93-138.

19  Sonaike, "Human Needs, Economic Development and Economic Nationalism: The African Case", Mimeo, University of Ife, Ile-Ife, 1978.
20  Olowoporoku, "ECOWAS: Some Unsettled Issues", *The Journal of Business and Social Studies*, (New Series), 1978.
21  Pinto and Knakal, "The Center-Periphery System Twenty Years Later", *Social and Economic Studies*, Vol. 22, No. 7, 1973.
22  Brown, *The Economics of Imperialism*, 1974; Fagan, "Cuban Revolutionary Politics", *Monthly Review*, Vol. 23, No. 11, 1972; Sears (ed.), *Cuba: The Economic and Social Revolution*, North Carolina University Press, 1964.
23  Olowoporoku and Sonaike, op. cit. 1977.

# Structural Dependency: The Nigerian Economy as a Case Study

B. C. SULLIVAN

*University of Nigeria, Nsukka, Nigeria*

STRUCTURAL DEPENDENCY THEORY has fast gained recognition as an alternative way to explain the current phase of underdevelopment in the L.D.Cs. Broadly the theory applies to the relationship between the rich and the poor nations of the world. It describes the dynamic on-going processes that create the conditions under which the centre nations are able to progressively exploit the periphery nations. Invariably what emerges is a dependent relationship which manifests various stages of transformations: colonialism, neo-colonialism and currently the domination by multi-nationals. The theory expresses frustration with the absence of a trickle down of the benefits from increases in G.N.P. as the development of an international complex of trading, financial and political relationships continues to deprive the periphery of the means to attain sustained economic growth.

In this paper we wish to examine the economic realities of Nigeria in the light of the claims of the dependency theory. As an L.D.C. country, Nigeria is an integral component of the periphery and as such is dependent upon the vagaries of International capitalism. A case study of Nigeria will be highly instructive.

### The Nature of Structural Dependency

The structural dependency argument claims to be a more plausible explanation of the growth and development dynamics of less developed economies than the traditional, neo-classical view which fundamentally asserts that economic development can be described in linear stages.[1] This model, which evolved in the decades following World War II, received wide-spread support from observers who argued that, after all, the advanced industrialized nations of the world all started from humble beginnings, with economies which were predominantly agrarian. More parallels have been drawn from the results of the application of the Marshall Plan. The achievements of those European nations who were recipients of aid under the Marshall Plan were put forward as an argument for increasing the level of financial aid flowing to the L.D.Cs.

Underdevelopment, it was argued, was a function of capital shortages. International organizations like The World Bank were used as the medium of massive transfers of funds to developing economies in an attempt to eliminate the severe capital constraints experienced by the L.D.Cs. However, in retrospect, we do not find that the massive shifts of financial resources from the industrialized to the non-industrialized world resulted in a rapid economic development. Reminiscent of Kenyesian fiscal theories and the Rostowian model that flows from it, the injection of substantial capital into L.D.Cs. has not activated the sleeping multiplier which in turn would generate a desired level of economic growth and development in the Third World countries.

The proponents of the Marshall Plan argument failed to recognize the fundamental structural differences that existed between nineteenth century Europe and twentieth century Third World economies. In nineteenth century Europe we witness a gradual transition from post-feudal society to industrial society with an almost parallel rate of population growth. But Third World transition in this century is not gradual. Certain features of Western society have been superimposed upon Third World economic and political structures with devastating effects. The importation of advanced sanitation and medical techniques into Third World countries has facilitated a population explosion of unanticipated magnitude—and in most countries the rate of economic growth lags behind the rate of population growth.

Despite its failures, classical theories of economic growth and development have not gone undefended. The neo-classical theorists, in their emphasis on a perfectly competitive model, now blame the institutional structures of L.D.Cs.—their state imposed constraints and market imperfections—for underdevelopment. They prescribe a policy package designed to remove market imperfections, arguing that a competitive market will be able to effectively perform its allocative function so that factors of production will receive a reward equivalent to their contributions to output. However, what the Neo-classicals fail to realize is that these institutional structures are often an outgrowth of the international capitalist system designed to make the periphery countries dependent upon and subservient to the needs and interests of the developed centre. The naivety of the neo-classical approach is clearly demonstrated by the impact of colonial economic policies which fostered inequality in the distribution of income and wealth.

Dependency theory seeks to overcome the inherent weakness of the neo-classical model by relating persistent inequality of social and economic dualism to the web of international relationships which has evolved as a result of colonial, neo-colonial and imperialistic policies. Resnik argues that there are three phases in the development of the relationship between the centre and the periphery countries.[2] The first phase was characterized by looting, plunder, and slavery, all of which facilitated massive capital accumulation in the centre countries. The second phase is characterized by the development of infrastructure in the periphery countries which facilitates colonial exploitation of a cheap labour supply on which the exports of raw materials and agricultural commodities depend. In the third phase we note the strategic positioning of multinational companies within the areas of abundant cheap labour and natural resources. By virtue of their size and concomitant economic power these multinationals are able to influence the policy decisions of governments in the periphery states.

Within most developing economies we find evidence of strongly dualistic structures. There is dualism in income distribution between the rural and urban areas; between the unskilled urban and rural labourer; and between regions of the same country. Dependency theorists have tended to pay more attention to international dualism than to domestic dualism.[3]

## Nigeria: A Development Experience

It is within the context of national and international dualism that we will examine the extent to which Nigeria can be said to be a dependent, peripheral economic system.

In 1946 the then colonial government of Nigeria introduced a ten year programme for development and social welfare for Nigeria. The programme offered investment opportunities to foreign businesses, mainly British, and by 1949 approximately 95 percent of Nigeria's import trade was in the hands of foreign businessmen.[4] This rapid consolidation of foreign investment became a major constraint on the development of indigenous enterprise. Further inhibitions arose from the enormous trade surpluses derived from the post-war export boom, surpluses which were absorbed by foreign merchants and the statutory marketing boards. Moreover, the greater proportion of the export earnings retained by the marketing boards were returned to and retained in Britain in the form of government securities and these amounted to £ 120 million in 1954 and £ 238 in 1961.

Indigenous business faced severe financial constraints throughout the 1950s and even in the post-independence sixties. Not only had foreign companies accumulated a fat surplus in the post-war boom, but they were also able to secure preferential treatment from the commerical banks for loan facilities since these banks were also owned by foreign capitalists. Externally generated finance from the major European banks was also accessible to Nigeria's foreign investors, thus virtually eliminating any possible ability to grow. It comes as no surprise then that the popular description of the Nigerian entrepreneur is one who is engaged in a small scale industry. As Carl Liedholm points out there is some evidence that certain types of manufacturing industries were actively discouraged by the colonial government.[5]

Before 1957 most foreign investments in Nigeria were in mining, retail, and wholesale trading.[6] After 1957, when the government came under Nigerian control, industrialization became a top-priority and the generous incentives and tariff protection offered induced further foreign investment in Nigeria. Despite constraints, indigenous entrepreneurs were successful in establishing a variety of enterprises, mainly in the fields of baking, tyreretreading, radio and T.V. assembly and others.[7] In general though, the growth of the young modern sector was dominated by, and attributable to, the preponderance of foreign investors. In 1966 for example private foreign investment accounted for a minimum of 70 per cent of total investment in basic industrial chemicals, food and soft drinks; and 60 per cent of the total in sugar, confectionary, brewing, textile, footwear, vegetable oil and food processing. Moreover the bulk of the services sector was dominated by foreign monopoly capital.

The absence of effective Nigerian entrepreneurship is partially explained by the preferences of the educated elite in Nigeria for a professional career, a career in the civil service, or employment with foreign firms. In consequence the potential innovative capacity of this section of the Nigerian population was inhibited by social attitudes and preferences. Even with independence international capitalism remained unchallenged. Political power was captured by the educated elite at independence and they, in collaboration with indigenous businessmen who had a vested interest in ensuring that foreign monopoly capital continued to profit in Nigeria, created an economic environment conducive to the continued growth of foreign investment. The so-called socialist policies of the era had no visible beneficial effect on the rural and urban masses. The rewards to the privileged elite were at best an appeasement that ensured the continued political stability necessary for the growth and prosperity of foreign capitalism in Nigeria. Foreign investment was justified on the grounds that the propensity to invest and the entrepreneurial ability of Nigerians would be assisted, rather than hindered, by the import of foreign capital.[8] This proposition turned out to be fallacious because foreign companies took full advantage of their monopoly power and economic incentives offered by the government and successfully stifled the growth of indigenous business.

1962 marked the beginning of an official policy that favoured indigenous entrepreneurs. The National Development Plan (1962-68) emphasized government intention to help indigenous businessmen. The 1968 Promulgation of Companies Decree furthered indigenization of the Nigerian economy by recognizing the need for more positive Nigerian participation in industrial development. The 1970-74 Development Plan carried this determination when it declared: "Specifically the federal government, in communication with the state governments, will ensure that certain industries, which are of basic and strategic importance to the economy, are effectively controlled by the public sector."[9] This policy statement became a political reality in 1972 with the proclamation of the Indigenization Decree, the first major attempt by government to wrest dominance of the Nigerian industrial sector out of the hands of foreign capitalism.

Why did Nigeria suddenly decide to reduce the degree of dependency on foreign capitalism when the composition of its ruling class was not vastly different to that of the preceding decade? The answer lies partly in the emergence of petroleum as the engine of development and in the political pressure emanating from the body of public opinion, which, better informed than in previous generations and with their confidence bolstered by a sagging post-civil war agricultural economy, exercised mounting pressure on the government to take more effective control of Nigeria's industrial sector.

The 1972 Nigerian Enterprises Promotion Decree, which replaced the Indigenization Decree promulgated early in the year, was designed to transfer ownership and control of the factors of production into indigenous hands.[10] The Decree specified those areas of industry where government would take over part of the equity of foreign owned companies. Twenty-five activities were specified in which Nigerians must henceforth have equity participation of not less than 40 per cent whilst 28 industrial and commerical ventures were reserved exclusively for Nigerians.[11] The 1972 decree was repealed by the Nigerian Enterprises Promotion Decree, 1977, to take effect from October 1978. By specifying 57 categories of business in which Nigerians must have a majority interest of at least 60 percent and the stipulation in Schedule III that the minimum indigenous equity participation must be 40 percent, the Decree guarantees extensive participation by Nigerians in their economy.

## Expatriate Management

The dearth of high level managerial skills in Nigeria brings us to another aspect of dependency. Nigeria is characterized by a hierarchical structure of management and administration, with expatriate labour at the pinnacle and indigenous labour employed at the middle and lower management and administration levels. This structure of skilled labour has been reinforced by the policies of multi-national corporations which tend to hold back the development of indigenous management skills, resulting in the increasing dependency of Nigeria on imported skilled and professional labour as the economy expands. The results of a survey conducted by the Nigerian Institute of Management, Enugu, showed that top flight expatriate management referred to "experience" as the major ingredient in their determination of whether or not a Nigerian was qualified to replace an expatriate. In contrast, the government stresses education and training, factors over which it has some control.

It can be argued that unless Nigerians are employed in executive, managerial positions, even as assistants, they can never acquire the "experience" demanded by the expatriate "bosses". Moreover, lack of "experience" can easily be used as a cover for job preferences for expatriate personnel, who themselves have no more "experience" than some Nigerians. There are also psychological barriers to the employment of Nigerians in responsible management positions since expatriate executives have traditionally been accustomed to employing Nigerians only in junior administrative or clerical positions and hence do not believe that Nigerians possess the innate mental or intellectual capacity to do justice to a post in top management. In a cross section study of 75 firms conducted in 1971, it was found that on average 3 per cent of the employees were expatriate, a national average. However, the study concluded that the ratio of expatriate labour to indigenous labour tended to understate the contribution made by expatriates since they usually held all or nearly all management posts.[12]

Employment of Nigerians in senior positions has often been referred to as "token" Nigerianization. There seems ample evidence to support this criticism. It has been found that Nigerians were often appointed to specially created posts and not to the traditional occupations of expatriate management. The posts of Personnel Officers and Public Relations Officers, previously classified as junior positions, are often upgraded to meet public demand for Nigerianization. Where Nigerians actually replaced an expatriate they were often given a portion of their predecessors' responsibility with the remainder being given to a new expatriate appointee. Data from the 1971 survey by the Nigerian Institute of Management shows that most firms intended to Nigerianize middle management by the mid-seventies but did not expect to do the same for top flight posts like Managing Director, General Manager, Financial or Marketing Directors.

A substantial evidence exists to support the thesis that dependency on expatriate executive management will continue for some time to come, mainly due to the policies of firms who appear to deliberately avoid the process of Nigerianization. For Nigeria to attain its objectives, it may be necessary for the government to force otherwise reluctant foreign companies to undertake to train top flight management and promote management assistants to top executive positions. The government could, when opportunities arise, transfer top flight Nigerian executives from the public sector to the private sector.

## Technological Dualism

The inability of indigenous entrepreneurs in Nigeria to invest in undertakings which require advanced technology results from externally imposed constraints. It has been suggested that non-Western norms and social values impede the acquisition of proper managerial and entrepreneurial dispositions by Nigerian entrepreneurs.[13] Contrary to this view, Harris and Rowe assert that Nigerians appear to be actively seeking material rewards and entrepreneurship, and as much of these as are socially honoured.[14]

The typical Nigerian entrepreneur is involved in enterprises which generally use a low level of technology. Shoe manufacturing, garment and baking industries are important examples. Import substitution industries often induce technological dependency by increasing the demand for imported raw or semi-processed materials.

The absence of a broad scientific base, typical of Black African countries, with Nigeria no exception, and the frailty of the existing legal framework in Nigeria have been additional constraints on technological development. In particular, the legal framework, full of loopholes, has enabled multi-national Corporations to effectively withhold technological information by prohibiting their foreign subsidiaries and branches from investigations that could lead to the development and application of competitive technology in the periphery. The experience of India is instructive. It has been found that foreign corporations operating in India maintained strict control over the use of their techniques by indigenous firms.[15]

Technological dualism results from international dependency and creates industrial enclaves in developing countries. An examination of Nigeria's trade components suggests that the manufacturing companies in Nigeria usually purchase extremely expensive machinery although inadequate advice often results in the wrong type of equipment in terms of efficiency and optimality. Moreover, subsidiary companies of international concerns in Nigeria have been found to procure equipment from their parent companies at twice the world market price with all the consequences for Nigerian foreign exchange reserves. There are examples where second hand equipment, with two-thirds of its life expired, were bought at the price of new equipment.[16]

The continued dependency by Nigeria on foreign technology imposes tremendous social and economic costs on the process of development. Firstly, there is the effect on income distribution. Capital intensive techniques usually result in the employment of a preponderance of highly skilled and professional classes who also earn a greater share of the national income. This in turn has an effect on consumption patterns, which are essentially imported luxury goods. Secondly, the urban style labour organizations, labour relations and remuneration systems of Western capitalism are imposed in Nigeria, thus further skewing income distribution between urban and rural areas and between the skilled and the unskilled workers. Finally, as Nigeria pursues its massive programme of educational expansion to satisfy the aspirations of those individuals who associate education with material success, there is a strong possibility of an over-production of educated elites who, as in India, might be dysfunctional to the economy and increase its dependency.

## Economic Growth and Income Distribution

A decade or more of rapid economic growth in L.D.Cs. has been of little benefit to perhaps a third of their population. Although the average per capita income of the Third World has increased by 50 per cent since 1960, this growth has been very unequally distributed among countries, regions within countries, and socio-economic groups.[17] While economic growth in the L.D.Cs. has increased inequality of income distribution among the people, there is evidence to suggest that in the centre countries income inequality has been significantly reduced.

Before the Nigerian civil war of 1967-70, the ratio of G.N.P. to G.D.P. declined from 99.5 per cent to 97.5 per cent, and the decline tended to be a continual one. Projections from the 1970-74 Plan period indicated a continued decline with a projected average ratio of 91.4 per cent.[18] The declining ratio can be attributed to the increasing participation by non-nationals in Nigeria's development and the leakages that result from salary remittances.

*Table I*

Annual Growth Rate of G.N.P. per capita by Region
and Country 1970-75

| Region and Country | G.N.P. per capita (1974 U.S.A. dollars) | | Annual growth rate (recent) | | |
|---|---|---|---|---|---|
| | 1950 (1) | 1975 (2) | 1950/60 (3) | 1960/70 (4) | 1970/75 (5) |
| Africa | 170 | 308 | 2.4 | 2.2 | 2.8 |
| Cameroun | 133 | 246 | 1.5 | 4.4 | -0.3 |
| Egypt, Arab Rep. of | 203 | 286 | 0.9 | 1.6 | 1.4 |
| Ethiopia | 358 | 94 | 2.3 | 2.7 | 0.5 |
| Ghana | 354 | 427 | 1.9 | -0.7 | -0.1 |
| Ivory Coast | 283 | 460 | -0.0 | 4.3 | 1.3 |
| Kenya | 129 | 200 | 1.0 | 3.2 | 2.5 |
| Liberia | N.A. | 377 | N.A. | 1.1 | 0.0 |
| Nigeria | 150 | 287 | 2.1 | 0.4 | 3.8 |
| Rhodesia/Zimbabwe | N.A. | 499 | N.A. | 0.7 | 2.6 |
| Senegal | 238 | 341 | 4.4 | -1.6 | 1.1 |
| Sudan | 118 | 267 | 2.7 | -0.7 | 15.4 |
| Tanzania | 84 | 160 | 3.7 | 3.0 | 0.6 |
| Uganda | 195 | 229 | 0.8 | 3.0 | -3.1 |
| Zaire | 94 | 139 | 1.1 | 2.4 | 1.1 |
| Zambia | 310 | 445 | 2.7 | 3.2 | -0.5 |
| *O.E.C.D. countries* | | | | | |
| O.E.C.D Countries | 2378 | 5238 | 3.0 | 4.1 | 2.3 |
| Canada | 3374 | 6112 | 1.2 | 3.7 | 3.2 |
| France | 2064 | 5294 | 3.5 | 4.3 | 3.2 |
| Germany, Federal Rep. of | 2005 | 6080 | 6.8 | 3.7 | 1.7 |
| Japan | 659 | 4105 | 7.3 | 9.4 | 4.3 |
| U.K. | 2064 | 3532 | 2.4 | 2.3 | 2.1 |
| U.S.A. | 3954 | 6495 | 1.5 | 3.3 | 1.7 |
| South Africa | 696 | 1211 | 1.7 | 3.2 | 1.8 |

Source: David Morawetz, *Twenty-Five Years of Economic Development 1950-75,* Johns Hopkins
University Press, 1977, pp. 77-80.

Table I shows the annual growth rate of G.N.P. per capita for selected
African countries and for the major industrial countries of the world. It helps
us to make objective comparisons between Nigeria and selected African countries and between Nigeria and the O.E.C.D. countries. Between 1950-60, the
growth rate for Nigeria's economy, at 2.1 per cent, was very close to the
average for all African countries at 2.4 per cent. The average for O.E.C.D.
countries was 3.0 per cent. Between 1960 and 1970 the annual average growth
rate for Nigeria fell to 0.4 per cent compared with 2.2 per cent for Africa as a
whole and 4.1 per cent for O.E.C.D. countries, thus underlining the increasing income disparity between the rich and the poor nations. An improvement
is noted for Nigeria in the period 1970-75 when its growth per capita was 3.8

compared with only 2.8 for Africa and 2.3 for O.E.C.D. countries. The improvement is largely due to rapid and major escalations in the price of crude oil between 1973-75. While these price increases benefited the major oil exporting countries, including Nigeria, they induced a major slowdown in the economies of the industrial West and Japan that led to disastrous consequences for most African economies.

The growth of the Nigerian economy in the past decade, in terms of G.N.P., has been impressive. If G.N.P. per capita were to continue to increase at the same rate for the next decade, would this necessarily result in an increase in material well-being of the mass of the Nigerian population? We have empirical evidence that supports the thesis that income inequality in Nigeria is not only widespread but growing. A huge disparity exists between the salaries of high level manpower and the wages received by unskilled labourers. For example, after 1971 the ratio of a messenger's pay to that of a Permanent Secretary (a top civil servant) was 1:30 compared to 1:12 in the United Kingdom. Nigeria's salary structure is typical of the pattern of income distribution in the L.D.Cs. The differentials in Nigeria are further exacerbated by the absence of an adequate state or government framework for the administration of social welfare and the existence of generous perquisites for managerial and professional workers.

The pattern of income distribution that now exists in Nigeria has its roots in colonial policy. The emphasis was on low wages and the sociological view of the African was that he was a "target worker", a thesis that received intellectual support from the now challenged, if not discredited, theory of "backward bending supply curve of labour". The policy of wage supervision for African workers continued throughout colonial rule and was inherited by independence governments who have shown greater interest in income distribution than the colonial government. Nigerian efforts in reducing disparities in wage income are instructive. Using the ratio of top salaries paid to civil servants to general wages paid to labourers, we find a steady improvement from: 1:43.5 in 1954; 1:38.2 in 1964; 1:30.4 in 1971; and 1:12.6 in 1974.[19]

The existing disparity between average incomes in the urban sector and those in the agricultural sector give the government cause for concern. It is within the agricultural sector that we find the most chronic manifestations of underdevelopment. The situation in the agrarian sector is compounded by the restless migration of the young to urban areas where they desperately search for employment. As a result incomes in the agricultural sector are actually falling because of the reduction in output, exacerbating further the inequality between average urban and average rural incomes. Hollis Chenery argues that only by pursuing a vigorous incomes policy in the agricultural sector will income inequality be effectively reduced.[20]

## Conclusion

Throughout this paper we have tried to present evidence to show that Nigeria is an integral component of periphery countries which are totally or partially dependent upon those few Western capitalist economies which constitute the centre.

We have seen that the parasitic activities of multi-national and transnational corporations tend to undermine developing economies. The proponents of large scale foreign investment argue that it leads to the spread of technological know-how and managerial skills. The limited transfers of technology to Nigeria, except in the oil sector, challenge the claims of the supporters of foreign monopoly capital. We find that the institutional and legal frameworks in Nigeria, because of their inherent weakness, have aided large foreign companies more than they have protected Nigerian economic interests.

In the past decade, successive Nigerian governments have struggled to reduce Nigeria's dependency by introducing various indigenization decrees. Few multi-national companies welcomed the changes. Those who accepted the changes did so grudgingly and many have searched desperately for loop-holes in the legislation. A few like the International Business Machines (IBM) requested the Federal Government for an exemption, which was rightly refused. Two other American interests, the First National City Bank of New York and the Colgate Palmolive, had to wind up their Nigerian businesses in 1977 in protest of the decree.

Programs and policies which are designed to disengage a poor country from dependency should not necessarily lead it away from the path of interdependency. Because of its enormously rich natural resources, Nigeria can afford to disengage its economy from the burdens of the colonial past and build an economic system which is committed to the principles of fair income distribution while providing enough incentives for its entrepreneurs.

## BIBLIOGRAPHY

AKEREDOLU-ALE, E. O. "The 'Competitive Threshold' Hypothesis and Nigeria's Industrialization Process: A Review Article." *Nigerian Journal of Economic and Social Studies* 14 (1972): 109-20.

ANYANWU, E. A. "Contributions of Finance to Industrial Development." In *Public Finance, Planning and Economic Development: Essays in Honour of Ursula Hicks.* Edited by W. L. David. London: Macmillan, 1973.

BARCLAYS Bank of Nigeria. "A Guide For Overseas Exporters and Prospective Investors in Nigeria." Lagos, 1976.

BAUER, P. T. *West African Trade: A Study of Competition, Oligopoly and Monopoly in a Changing Economy.* London: Routledge and K. Paul, 1963.

CHENERY, HOLLIS B. "The Structural Approach to Development Policy." *American Economic Review* LXV (1975):301-16.

CHENERY, HOLLIS B., et al. *Redistribution With Growth.* Published for the World Bank by Oxford University Press, 1974.

EKUKINAN, A. E. "Economic Revolution That Is Becoming." *Nigerian Trade Journal* 24 (1977).

HARRIS, J. R. and ROWE, M. P. "Entrepreneurial Pattern in the Nigerian Sawmilling Industry." *Nigerian Journal of Economics and Social Studies,* 1966.

KIDRON, MICHAEL. *Foreign Investment in India.* Oxford University Press, 1965.

LEIDHOLM, C. "The Influence of Colonial Policy on the Growth and Development of Nigeria's Industrial Sector." In *Growth and Development of the Nigerian Economy.* Edited by Carl Eicher and C. Leidholm. Michigan State University Press, 1970.

MORAWETZ, D. *Twenty-five Years of Economic Development 1950-75.* Johns Hopkins University Press, 1977.

Nigeria, Federal. *Second National Development Plan 1970-74.* Lagos, 1970.

——. *Third National Development Plan 1975-80.* Lagos, 1975.

Nigerian Institute of Management. "Indigenization and Management in Nigeria." Enugu, Nigeria, 1971. (Mimeographed.)

OYEJIDE, T. A. "Patterns of Economic Growth in Nigeria 1957-67." In *Tariff Policy and Industrialization in Nigeria.* Nigeria: Ibadan University Press, 1975.

RESNIK, S. A. "State of Development Economics." *American Economic Review* LXV (1975): 317-22.

SINGER, H. W. "Dualism Revisited: A New Approach to the Problems of Dual Society in Developing Countries" *Journal of Development Studies* VII (1970).

THOMAS, B. D. *Capital Accumulation and Technology Transfer: A Comprehensive Analysis of Nigerian Manufacturing Industries.* New York: Praeger, 1975.

TODARO, M. P. *Economic Development in the Third World.* London: Longmans, 1977.

## NOTES

1  Todaro, *Economic Development in the Third World,* London, Longmans, 1977.

2  Resnik, "State of Development Economies," *American Economic Review,* vol. LXV, No. 2, 1975, pp. 317-22.

3  Singer, "Dualism Revisited: A New Approach to the Problems of Dual Society in Developing Countries," *Journal of Development Studies,* Vol. VII, 1970, p. 60.

4  Bauer, P. T., *West African Trade: A Study of Competition, Oligopoly and Monopoly in a Changing Economy,* London, Routledge and K. Paul, 1963.

5  Liedholm, "The Influence of Colonial Policy on the Growth and Development of Nigeria's Industrial Sector", in Eicher and Liedholm (eds.), *Growth and Development of the Nigerian Economy,* Michigan State University Press, 1970, p. 52.

6  Oyejide, "Patterns of Economic Growth in Nigeria: 1957-67," in *Tariff Policy and Industrialization in Nigeria,* Ibadan University Press, 1975, p. 21.

7  Anyanwu, "Contribution of Finance to Industrial Development", in W. L. David (ed.), *Public Finance and Planning Economic Development: Essays in Honour of Ursula Hicks,* London, Macmillan, 1973, p. 71.

8  Akeredolu-Ale, "The 'Competitive Threshold' Hypothesis and Nigeria's Industrialization Process: A Review Article," *Nigerian Journal of Economic and Social Studies,* 1972, p. 116.

9  Nigeria, Federal, *Development Plan (1970-74),* Lagos, 1970, p. 146.

10  Barclays Bank of Nigeria, "A Guide for Overseas Exporters and Prospective Investors in Nigeria", Lagos, 1977, p. 3.

11  Nigeria, Federal, *Third National Development Plan (1975-80),* Lagos, 1975, p. 19.

12  Nigerian Institute of Management, "Indigenization and Management in Nigeria", Enugu, 1972, p. 17 (MSS).

13  Ekukinan, "Economic Revolution That Is Becoming", *Nigerian Trade Journal,* Vol. 24, No. 1, 1977.

14  Harris and Rowe, "Entrepreneurial Patterns in the Nigerian Sawmilling Industry", *Nigerian Journal of Economics and Social Studies,* 1966, p. 94.

15  Kidron, *Foreign Investment in India,* Oxford University Press, 1965, p. 282.

16  Thomas, *Capital Accumulation and Technology Transfer: A Comprehensive Analysis of Nigerian Manufacturing Industries,* New York, Praeger, 1975, p. 50.

17  Chenery, et al., *Redistribution With Growth,* London, Oxford University Press, 1974, p. 13.

18  Nigeria, Federal, *The Second National Development Plan (1970-74)*, Lagos, 1970, p. 46.
19  Ratios based on calculations by L.C. Ezeauku from his unpublished M.Sc. Thesis, University of Nigeria.
20  Chenery, "The Structural Approach to Development Policy," *American Economic Review*, Vol. LXV, No. 2, 1975, p. 310.

# PART II

# CULTURAL ASPECTS OF DEPENDENCY

# Ideological Dependency and the Problem of Autonomy in Nigeria

UZODINMA NWALA

*University of Nigeria, Nsukka, Nigeria*

IDEOLOGY COULD BE INTERPRETED as a system of ideas. This is true in a sense; but to delimit it in this way is to leave it in the realm of abstraction.

All ideologies have social roots and every ideology is a system of ideas which expresses a social reality that is independent of the perception which its cultural bearers or analysts may have of it.[1] At the base of this social reality is the economic structure of a society. Man is essentially definable in terms of his activities. Aristotle missed this point when he defined man as essentially a rational being. The fact is that man is essentially a being that produces. Man maintains his being through his productive activities. Man has both rational and irrational qualities—and each quality is reflected in his productive behaviours. We understand man better not by abstracting and glorifying his rationality but through the study and comprehension of his productive activity which is often contradictory. As man lives through continuous productive activity, we can sum up and define man's being as a dialectical process uniting two opposites at the base of which is his productive activity.

What is social about man is his relationship with others in the productive process. This makes society a system of productive relations rather than of ideas.

An important element of man's activities is his capacity to think and grasp his actions, including "thinking his own thought" as philosophers do. This process produces and reproduces a system of ideas. But the system of ideas is only a reflection of man's social activities, not reality itself. Frederick William G. Hegel erred by mystifying the "Idea" and positing it as "Reality itself". While Aristotle falsely takes one side of this ideational process (rational) as reality and proceeds to define man as a "rational being", Hegel, in attempting to unify the two opposites, *ideas* and *reality*, still held on to them as *ideas*. Hegel did recognise that idea has an intimate relationship with social reality, but he turned the relationship upside down, positing that prior ideas are superior to social reality. Because of his respect for Aristotle as well as for God and the whole of Western religious and philosophical tradition, Hegel ended up proclaiming this dialectical and contradictory process as ultimately Rational—a proposition that transformed Idea into Reason as well.

In this century, Max Weber, following the same philosophical preoccupation with "thinking", "ideas", and "ideology", proclaimed the capitalist system as essentially rational.

Ideologies are class centred. They can be rational or irrational depending on the class interests and the social reality represented. For example capitalism is rational to the capitalist but certainly irrational to the worker and the oppressed strata of society. The former finds that their interests and being are realized by the system, but the latter finds their interests and being negated by the same system.

## Class Character of Social Systems: Ideological Dependence

We asserted that each social system has its corresponding class ideology. What we refer to as the social system or a national entity is actually the dominant social formation in a society which manifests itself in the dominant mode of production and productive relations in that society. Alongside with it are subordinate social formations. For example, within the peripheral capitalist system in Nigeria there are communal and feudal social formations which are dominated by the capitalist class. The tendency is for the dominant class to annihilate some of the elements of the subordinate classes and absorb others, both their material and ideological dimensions.[2] Each social system is maintained and sustained by the class or people whose interests it serves. Thus, the feudal system serves the interests of the feudal lords and their agents. The dominant ideology is imposed more or less on those strata of society whose interests and being are negated by the system. The ruling class endeavors at the same time to feed them with the ideologies of this system. The result is that the subordinate classes are ideologically and materially dependent on the ruling class.

The great achievements of world capitalism resulted in the break up of the traditional national frontiers and the establishment of a complex structure of economic and political relationships among the nations of the world. One important result of this development is the international division of labour and specialization; but its character and direction as well as the dynamics of change have been determined mainly by the centre of world capitalism, which today includes the West European countries, U.S.A. and Japan. Built around this centre are the peripheral regions—the Third World countries in Asia, Africa and Latin America—which are structurally related to the centre in a subordinate way. Development within this peripheral region is determined by the interests of the centre of world capitalism rather than the logic and realities at the periphery or their fundamental domestic interests.

The centre-periphery relationship is more easily grasped when we analyze the structure of the economies of both the central and peripheral regions and examine the historical process leading to this structural dependency. Such an historical analysis reveals that the peripheral regions are indeed part of a world social structure which, according to Samir Amin, "...form a structured, hierarchical totality", dominated by the "great absentee member" of colonial society: "the dominant metropolitan bourgeoisie".[3]

## Ideologically Dependent Nigeria

In our introductory remarks on ideology and social system, we emphasized the fact that social systems express particular ideologies and that neither can be studied in isolation. In actual fact no ideology can be concretely grasped without locating it within the social context which it expresses. Even the non-Marxist scholars recognise that ideas have certain relationship with the environment. However, they fail to understand the dialectical relationship between them, and only posit the relationship in a static and mechanical form.

To analyse Nigeria's ideological dependency, we need to study the character and the evolution of the social system we have in Nigeria. But what do we mean when we talk about the Nigerian ideology? We mean the system of ideas—political, economic, religious, legal, philosophical, artistic—which shapes the dominant social system we have in Nigeria. Although the pre-capitalist social formations—communalism and feudalism—still persist in certain regions of the country, yet they all bow to the logic of industrial, commercial and finance capital which dominates the whole social framework of this country. The class whose interest is served by this system is the bourgeois class. The 1976 Draft Constitution and the proceedings of the Constituent Assembly—the basis for the legal charter for Nigeria for generations to come—bear the imprint of the interests of this class. In more concrete terms, the struggle between this class, which includes the military and the bureaucratic elite, and the feudal class in our society has resulted in the increasing elimination of the privileges and power of the latter. The Local Government Reforms, the new Land Policy and the decisions of the Constituent Assembly to scrap the House of Chiefs are all eloquent testimonies of the power of the bourgeoisie and the increasing crystallization of the class-character of our society.

Nigeria's economic system has been described as a mixed economy[4] which implies a mixture of socialism and capitalism. We must reject this conception because the State enterprises which define the "socialist element" of this mixed economy are in fact established to aid private accumulation by the capitalist class. The so-called "state enterprises" are not run on socialist principles, do not serve the interest of workers, but rather serve that of capital. Furthermore, they are operated mainly by private contractors and managed by the members and clients of the bourgeois class. For the public sector to become a socialist sector and serve the interests of the workers,

"... its relations of production must change to favour labour over capital, its mode of production and distribution must be socialist, it must operate under socialist norms and symbols and it must be propelled by the desire to satisfy the basic needs and traditional consumption habits of the population rather than by the profit motive."[5]

The historical origin of Nigeria's mixed economy ideology goes back to the activities of the British finance oligarchy in Nigeria. In Nnoli's views:

> This oligarchy could not operate its profitable colonial enterprises without some other activities which were not capable of yielding profits. During the early colonial period profitable enterprises were largely possible in import-export trade, banking, insurance, shipping, wholesale and retail trades and tin mining. The finance oligarchies concentrated their economic activities in these areas. But railways and roads were important for these enterprises; so was the mining of coal to be used in running the railway system. Similarly, electricity, telephone and telegraph, the civil service, the army and police were important. The colonial state intervened to provide these services using the taxes obtainable from the colonized.

> This is the historical origin of the public sector in the Nigerian economy. It is a sector that is based on the inability of its enterprises to generate profit, that services the sector that is profitable to the finance oligarchy, that does not service the interests of the colonized but is paid for by their taxes. Therefore, it was an instrument for the exploitation which occurs at the place of work. It reflects the super-exploitation of the colonized. And because it was only peripheral to the interests of the finance oligarchy, conditions of work in it, particularly the wages, were less attractive than in the private companies, with a consequent lowering of worker morale and productivity. These consequences are in turn used to discredit public ownership of economic activities.[6]

Awa confirms Nnoli's thesis when he writes:

> "Capitalist ideology has been the root of all social and political activities (in Nigeria), and it was carried over after the imperialists made their formal exits. The main concern of capitalism has been to develop the economy and to assure maximum returns to private enterprise. The bourgeois elements and the traditional elites who took over power revelled in their glory and competed bitterly over the sectional control of the country's resources."[7]

## Neo-Colonialism

We can isolate three conditions which foster neo-colonialism. First, the existence of a capitalist system in a colonial society provides the framework for neo-colonialism.

Second, the colonial powers must create economic structures, production and distribution relations through which class interests can crystallize and a value system, backed with strong economic rewards for the participants in the system.

Third, the creation of a bourgeois class of merchants, industrialists, finance magnets—bankers, insurance agents, stock-brokers, landlords, military brass, and the bureaucrats—as well as the petty-bourgeois class of professionals, intellectuals, business executives, mass media executives, whose class interests coincide with those of international monopoly capitalism brings about a neo-colonialist society.

The present structure of the Nigerian economy is based on a relationship which enables the imperialist forces to maintain control of the economic and political developments in Nigeria. It is an economic system linked peripherally to the centre of world capitalism with the Nigerian merchant, industrial, and financial interests—now assisted by the military-bureaucratic alliance running the government—acting as the agents of foreign capitalists who continue to exploit Nigeria's wealth. These neo-colonial agents were reared under colonialism whose interests they still serve. According to Jack Woddis:

> While colonialism meant the direct political and economic domination of one country by another, on the basis of state power being in the hands of the colonial power, it was never solely a question of foreign rule, but rather that of foreign rule allied with certain economic and political strata of the indigenous people which had an interest in supporting colonialism. Thus colonialism was an alliance between the occupying power and the internal forces of conservation and tradition.[8]

Nigeria's traditional rulers—Emirs, Obas, Obis, and Chiefs—who depended on the colonial powers for political support and their material needs and in turn ensured the continuation of traditional ideas and religions also acted as agents of the colonial administration in their various localities. In the new political order that emerged after independence, the traditional rulers have lost political and economic power to a new elite who are men and women who owe their status to formal education which paradoxically ties them to imperial interests and value systems. It is not surprising that a former Governor-General of Nigeria, Sir Hugh Foot (now Lord Caradon) would describe Samuel Adebo, a former top government civil servant as among modern Africans "trained in the traditions of the British civil service," whose "outlook and methods and instincts come from that training" and who "are English not only in their training but also in their attitude to public affairs."[9] The colonial economic system bred petty capitalists—merchants, industrialists and financiers—who depend on foreign companies and also serve their economic interest.

The Nigerian army is a colonial army reared in the traditions of British military system and generally tied to Britain both in sympathy and in ideas. The educational system introduced in the country was aimed at infusing the cultural values of the metropolis and the destruction of indigenous culture and values. Similarly, through several instruments of social control, Nigerians have remained victims of foreign domination materially and spiritually. For example, the mass media in Nigeria "tend to operate more subtly and benignly in importing new, predominantly foreign, values which may be technical, religious, commercial and consumptionist, propagandist and immoral."[10] Similarly the religious bodies "specialize in the internationalization of morals and ethics thereby controlling men's minds and ensuring a high degree of conformity to values, beliefs and traditions often imposed in society by the dominant class."[11]

Eteng has described the unity of ideology and the material and economic foundations of the Nigerian society which finds expression in the process of socialization where technical rationality has become substantive rationality. According to him:

> A major trend of importance indicates that modern socialization processes which were basically introduced by past colonial and capitalist brigands through the instrumentality of their supportive missionaries, and improved upon and expanded by subsequent national

governments, now wholly determine the main profile of the Nigerian political economy. In particular, modern socialization patterns directly or indirectly determine (a) the member, sex and age composition of, as well as types of skills and techniques possessed, and the personality characteristics manifested by members of the Nigerian labour force; (b) the creative and productive capacities of various occupational categories among Nigerians, (c) the number of specific job openings available, or the rate of unemployment, in any one given time in the country; (d) types of work organizations and their country-wide distribution; (e) systems of ranking workers within their respective work organizations; (f) variations and differentials in salaries, emoluments and benefits accruing to workers; (g) the nature and rate of career progression in different work situations; (h) work attitudes and habits; (i) consumption habits and styles of various classes in Nigeria and (j) the general attitude of Nigerians to life and death.[12]

## Consequences of Ideological Dependency and Domination

Oni and Onimode have examined the consequences of a neo-colonial dependency for Nigeria. These consequences may be summarized in five propositions.[13]

(1) Economic surplus is left in foreign hands. According to Oni and Onimode,

> Foreign domination means foreign control and foreign appropriation of our national economic surplus. It is this national surplus value in the form of profits of all private and public enterprises in Nigeria that we need to re-invest in order to expand and diversify production in manufacturing, agriculture, mining, and similar activities. This is what we need to increase our rate of investment in or to offer jobs to our unemployed masses, as well as to expand and improve our education, health, transport, water, electricity and other services. The profits of the foreign enterprises can be mobilised for our self-reliant development and for terminating our hopeless dependence on increasingly exploitative and masochistic foreign 'aid' and foreign investment. This national economic surplus is the life-blood, the engine of development of any national economy. For as long as foreigners own and control our national resources, for that long will they continue to appropriate and export the surplus or profits accruing from utilization of these resources for their own development. It is this export of national surplus from the Third World by world capitalism that makes the advanced capitalist countries get richer while we get abysmally poorer. *The advanced capitalist countries can only continue to be so much richer than us for as long as we agree to remain so much poorer, by allowing them to dominate our national economy and appropriate our national economic surplus.*[14]

(2) Comprehensive planning becomes impossible because the actual control of the production and distribution of the country's wealth is in foreign hands.

(3) Political stability and sovereignty is undermined.

(4) National independence is a farce.

(5) Mass misery and cultural perversion may result.

Samir Amin agrees with these propositions and observes that "...the center plays active role, opening up the market of the periphery in accordance with its own purpose."[15]

An ideologically dependent Nigeria cannot operate a self-reliant economy. It is obvious that the conditions of material and ideological dependency make for underdevelopment, lead to exploitation of a country's resources, make for wasteful consumption and gross inequalities in the distribution of a country's wealth and income. It maintains foreign domination.

For Nigeria to regain autonomy over her economic, social and political life, she must first break her ties with world monopoly capitalism in which she is only a convenient appendage. The neo-colonial character of our social system cannot be abolished without first abolishing the capitalist system. And this implies a social revolution and not just the reformation of the socio-political order. Reform programmes, whatever their character and no matter their leadership, are bound to fail within a neo-colonial, capitalist system.

## BIBLIOGRAPHY

AMIN, SAMIR. *Accumulation on a World Scale. A Critique of the Theory of Underdevelopment.* New York: Monthly Review Press, 1974.

AWA, EME. "The Place of Ideology in Nigerian Politics." *African Review* 4 (1974):358-364.

ETENG, INYA A. "Changing Patterns of Socialization and their Impact on National Development in Nigeria." Unpublished lecture, General Studies 103, University of Nigeria, Nsukka, n.d.

FOOT, HUGH. "Teaching the Nations to Live." *The Observer Week-end Review*, 3 February 1963.

HEGEL, G. W. F. *Science of Logic.* Translated by A. V. Miller, London: George Allen and Urwin Ltd., 1969.

Nigeria, Federal Republic of. *Report of the Constitutional Drafting Committee Containing the Draft Constitution.* Lagos: Federal Ministry of Information, 1976.

NNOLI, OKWUDIBA. "The Ideological Foundations of the Nigerian Draft Constitution 1976." *The Comrade.* Nsukka: University of Nigeria, February 1977.

ONI, COMRADE OLA and ONIMODE, BADE. *Economic Development of Nigeria: The Socialist Alternative.* Ibadan: The Nigerian Academy of Arts, Sciences and Technology, 1975.

WODDIS, JACK. *Introduction to Neo-Colonialism: The New Imperialism in Asia, Africa and Latin America.* New York: International Publishers, 1967.

## NOTES

1  The distinction between ideology as an expression of social reality and ideology as "an expression of the same reality but as perceived by people" is merely theoretical. Every ideology is someone's perception of social reality. However, social reality is always perceived from a certain perspective. It is this perspective that needs to be stressed. Thus the bourgeoisie perceive their world differently from the way the oppressed strata of society perceive the same world. Nigeria's new land tenure policy is being perceived differently by the feudal elements from the way the bourgeoisie or even the exploited Nigerian mass perceive it.

2  Hegel, *Science of Logic*, London, 1969, p. 107.

3  Amin, *Accumulation on A World Scale. A Critique of the Theory of Underdevelopment*, New York, Monthly Review Press, 1974, vol. 11, p. 360.

4  Nigeria, Federal Republic of, *Report of the Constitutional Drafting Committee Containing the Draft Constitution*, Lagos, Federal Ministry of Information 1976, vol. 1, p. xiii.

5  Nnoli, "The Ideological Foundations of the Nigerian Draft Constitution 1976", *The Comrade*, University of Nigeria, Nsukka, no. 1 February 1977, p. 10.

6  Nnoli, Ibid.

7  Awa, "The Place of Ideology in Nigerian Politics," *African Review*, vol. 4, No. 3 1974, pp. 358-364, 380.

8  Woddis, *Introduction to Neo-Colonialism: The New Imperialism in Asia, Africa and Latin America*, New York, International Publishers, 1967, pp. 24-25.

9  Hugh Foot, "Teaching the Nations to Live," *The Observer Week-end Review*, February 3, 1963.

10   Eteng, "Changing Patterns of Socialization and their Impact on National Development in
     Nigeria," Unpublished Lecture, *General Studies 103,* University of Nigeria, Nsukka.
11   Eteng, Ibid.
12   Eteng, Ibid.
13   Oni and Onimode, *Economic Development of Nigeria: The Socialist Alternative,* Ibadan, The
     Nigerian Academy of Arts, Sciences and Technology, 1975, pp. 10-12.
14   Oni and Onimode, Ibid., p. 10.
15   Amin, *Accumulation on a World Scale,* 1974, pp. 160-302.

# Educational Strategy for Cultural Independence in West Africa

*University of Nigeria, Nsukka, Nigeria*

Economic AND TECHNOLOGICAL DEPENDECY has received so much emphasis in development literature that we have almost ignored cultural dependency. In a world which measures welfare, quality of life and the comparative status of nations by the visible and tangible technological and economic achievements, it is not surprising that cultural problems would be relegated to a marginal position in the debate on development and under-development. This technological bias ignores the immediate relationship between technological and economic development and cultural process. An understanding of dependency is impossible unless we take its cultural content into serious consideration.

A critical assessment of the history of relationships between the industrial nations and the West African countries since the colonial era—the basis of present dependency—indicates that such interactions involved more than technological and economic elements. They had important cultural dimensions of which the colonial educational system has had the most dysfunctional impact on our cultures. Probably the most pernicious effect is the predisposition among educated West Africans to uncritically accept and adopt Western cultural norms and values as universally valid. The acquisition of formal education was confused with Westernization. Educational policies and practices directly or indirectly supported efforts to assimilate colonized people culturally. Post-colonial educational systems and practices have reinforced colonial traditions and Westernization policy thus leading to further alienation and cultural dependency. Westernization, therefore, appears to be a *conditio sine qua non* for biased international relations and for economic dependency.

## The Political Ideology of Education

Education is never politically and ideologically neutral. No matter how it is interpreted and conceived, education is always a social institution which expresses the socio-political intentions, aspirations and interests of the dominant social groups in a society. It always entails indoctrination and moral suasion; and emphasizes discipline, obedience and conformity. An educational system necessarily fulfills contradictory roles. It enables society to provide the technical skills needed for the proper performance of specific functions and duties; and in the transmission of socio-cultural values, the education mission is highly subjective in the sense that the products of education generally reflect the will and interests of the groups who control the educational policy. In its latter role, education becomes a tool with which generations are made "subservient" to a particular type of socio-economic and socio-political order. The ways technical skills acquired through the medium of education are put into the service of society are to a large extent dependent on what people are taught to believe through the same educational system. Notions of good and bad, adequate and unacceptable, and success and failure which determine human attitudes and condition the way people behave and use their talents and skills in the service of society are basically determined by education. Education is selective in principle and practice: it values some norms which society promotes through appropriate incentives, and it sanctions other interests and values which are not desired.

Policy statements on the aims of education are sometimes misleading. Both the "civilizing mission" of the colonial era and the post-colonial emphasis on a "development mission" are conceived to serve specific interests and purposes which are diametrically opposed to those of the people for whom they are designed to help. The colonial as well as the post-colonial educational policies are fundamentally nourished by the same group of ideas: the planned penetration of underdeveloped countries with a view to achieving economic, political, ideological, geopolitical, strategic, military, and diplomatic benefits for the industrial Western countries. The marginal changes that have occurred in the political status of West African countries have not changed this. After more than one and one-half decades of political independence, no fundamental modifications in the content, method and orientation have been made in the educational institutions inherited from the colonial past. We must differentiate between qualitative and quantitative types of change. While qualitative change deals with the contents, methods and ideological and political foundations of educational institutions, quantitative changes are basically concerned with the reproduction, multiplication and the diffusion of existing institutions whose qualitative design or contents are largely unchanged. West African countries are noted for their quantitative changes in education: more modern schools are being established to bridge educational gaps, to eradicate illiteracy, and in the best cases to produce skilled manpower in accordance with the requirements of the modern sector of the economy but the contents, methods, organization and fundamental orientation of the educational system are more or less the same as they were in the colonial era.

There is a serious time-lag between West African political transformation and the transformations of its educational systems. The policy of Africanizing the teaching profession through recruiting more highly trained and experienced teaching staff is not necessarily an indication of intellectual emancipation unless it is accompanied by appropriate teaching materials and programmes designed to emancipate Africans from foreign domination. It is an indictment of our political efforts of educational transformation that Patrick von Dias could still comment in 1970, ten years after political independence had been won in West Africa, that: "It is a fact that the contemporary educational systems being operated in (independent African countries) have been and still remain a product of the industrialized Western societies. Those systems are, therefore, bound to specific historical and social-cultural conditions of their emergence and further development."[1] This condition reflects the overall situation of the world-wide domination of African countries by industrial nations and points to a situation of master-servant relationship which biases educational undertakings in favour of the more powerful industrial nations at the obvious expense of African countries. It is in the light of this kind of lop-sided international relation, in which the interests of industrial nations command primacy, that the following statement by Hasso von Recum has its full significance: "In the (historical) process of transferring educational institutions of the (industrial) type into (non-industrial) countries, the sociological (and enviromental) aspects of the educational 'aid' very often remain under-developed."[2] The statement emphasizes the well-known fact that modern education as practised in developing countries tends

1. to dissociate itself from the objective conditions and realities of under-developed countries;
2. to be dominated by foreign facts and data, and
3. to divert the attention of students in underdeveloped countries from their own conditions of existence.

A functional link has been established between modern education as practised in developing countries and the general foreign policy of industrial nations. Richard Martinus Emge argues that

> ...foreign cultural (and educational) policy is, irrespective of the way one looks at it, always politics... In the field of foreign policy, one is confronted with an area of power struggles, competitions, antagonisms as well as of 'give and take' of a well meaning co-operation among nations. Foreign cultural (and educational) policy consequently remains, as a matter of principle and of fact, always an integral part of the overall foreign policy of a state, whether as part of its official diplomacy or not. It defines and applies to the indirect eminent political sphere of cultural diffusion as promoted by the state; it characterizes and relates to object of international agreements, contracts and organizations. It is, therefore, always subordinated to politics in its restricted sense; at least, it is tied up to politics in a strict, functionally circular way. The direction and orientation given to foreign cultural (and educational) activities and the contents (and methods) of such activities largely depend on the intentions pursued through the channel of international policy by a state.[3]

If domestic politics means the "struggle for the control of state decision-making power,"[4] foreign policy is necessarily the "aspiration towards sharing power or toward influencing power distribution among states on a foreign socio-economic and socio-political terrain."[5] Education is an important foreign policy instrument in the hands of a dominant power—foreign or domestic. "How to win friends and influence people (outside the state boundaries) and win people to their own way of thinking, and 'sell' oneself and one's ideas"[6] are important foreign policy goals which can be achieved without a military force but through cultural domination. While the use of military or police force to achieving long-term domination in international relations tends to arouse

the countervailing forces of hostile nationalism, a tactically well-conceived program of education is often well received but paradoxically it achieves the goal
of cultural domination.

Nations, like individuals, like to present their best image to other nations and peoples. This is the role of cultural education. There is also "image"
warfare among competing nations and the struggle between the capitalist
West and the socialist East for the control of the minds of developing countries
is a case in point. Both occur through the use of conventional mass media
and modern education—a mass educational institution having a lot in common with mass communication. As a matter of fact, modern classroom education, apart from being mostly unilateral in terms of communication and
authoritarian in terms of the sources of information, is divorced from feelings
and emotions. Arnold Toynbee compounds the European cultural arrogance
by lending his very high prestige to the prevailing myth in Europe that African
cultural achievements were not deserving of civilized respect.[7] This Eurocen-
tric view of cultural achievements held by industrial nations interested and involved in West Africa tends to lend validity to Jacob Viner's assertion that
"underdeveloped countries (in general and West Africa in particular) are to a
certain important degree pawns on the chessboard of international power
politics."[8]

We are led to the conclusion that the political aims of colonial policy and
their educational mission are complementary. As the former defined and set
the general colonial frame and order, it also determined the orientation of
educational activities which, in turn, served as one of the major instruments of
cultural penetration and domination. Maurice Delafosse made the same points
when he wrote:

> As we need translators and interpreters to make ourselves understood by the indigenes, we
> also need intermediaries belonging both to the indigenous cultural environments by the vir-
> tue of their birth and to the European cultural milieu by their education in order to make
> the indigenes appreciate and adopt this alien civilization against which they manifest a
> profound distaste which is difficult to overcome.[9]

Commenting on this, Abdou Moumouni observes:

> What it's all about is not only to foster economic exploitation of colonies as much as possi-
> ble, but also to enhance political domination by applying systematic and more complete
> measures of alienation to the people in the colonies and by keeping tnem in subjection with
> a view to securing their loyalty. In the context of such peculiar policy, a role of a first order
> devolved upon colonial education as a means of cultural oppression and of depersonaliza-
> tion.[10]

On his part, M. Brevie makes it clear that the aim of colonial education is
political and cultural dependency.

> The colonial duty as well as the political and economic necessities impose a double task on
> our educational work: on the one hand, it is a question of producing indigenous cadres who
> are destined to become our auxiliaries in all domains and of supporting the ascension of an
> elite carefully chosen. On the other hand, one has to educate the masses of the population in
> order to bring them closer to us and to transform their way of life... From a political point of

view, it is a matter of making indigenes aware of our efforts and intentions to tie them down to their own place while at the same time making them participate (peripherally) in the French way of life. From an economic point of view, it is a question of educating producers and consumers of tomorrow.[11]

For these reasons, M. Brevie says, "the content of our educational programmes is not merely a pedagogical issue and concern. The pupil (in the colony) is an (important) instrument of the local colonial policy."[12]

Colonial educational policy also espoused a utilitarian point of view. Gouverneur General Roume argued that education is necessarily "...a precious thing that one cannot but distribute sparingly."[13] The policy implication of his philosophy was clear enough: "Let us limit the favours of education to qualified beneficiaries."[14] Article 5 of the official Decree of 10 May 1924 defines what is meant by "qualified" with respect to the enrollment of Africans into institutions of learning: "The attendance of educational institutions is compulsory for the sons of chiefs and notabilities."[15] Gouverneur General Roume translated this definition into an enrollment policy:

Let us first select our pupils from among the sons of chiefs and notables; the indigenous society is highly stratified in a hierarchical order. The social classes are clearly determined by heredity and customs. It is on these classes that we base our authority in the administration of (the colonies); it is above all with them that we have a constant functional relation. The prestige connected with birth must be reinforced by the respect conferred by knowledge.[16]

Article 2 of the Decree of 10 May 1924 stipulates that "primary education has essentially to aim at bringing closer to us as large a number of indigenes as possible, at making them get familiarized with our language, our institutions and our methods, at leading them to economic and social progress through a prudent evolution of their own civilization." Article 32 of the Decree spells out the aims of an "advanced primary education" in each colony as:
— to provide a complement of instruction to sons of indigenous notables, sons who are called upon later to support our administration;
— to prepare candidates for the schools of the Central Government with a view to producing indigenous agents of general cadres; and
— to directly produce the agents of local cadres; the number and the character of the educational levels to promote will vary in accordance with the needs of the colony.

Article 64 provides that "French is the sole language allowed to be in use in schools. It is strictly forbidden that teachers communicate with their pupils in the language of the country."[17]

A wholesale export of French culture was not the only thing wrong with the French educational policy for West Africa. It was official policy to teach French cultural superiority and for African students to accept their cultural inferiority. The educational philosophy and programmes made these clear enough:

Through an education well conducted, the indigene should be made to appropriately locate his race and civilization *vis a vis* other races and civilizations past and present. It is an ex-

cellent way to attenuate this inborn vanity for which he has all along been blamed, to render
him more modest by inculcating in him a strong and reasoned loyalty... The entire teaching
of history, of geography, (of religion and morals) must tend to demonstrate that France is a
wealthy and mighty nation capable of making itself respected, and that it is at the same time
great and magnanimous for the nobleness of sentiments and generosity, a nation that has
never retreated while confronted with huge human and financial sacrifices meant to deliver
and protect enslaved people and to bring to savage people peace, the benefits of
civilization.[18]

We have presented enough evidence from official statements to support
our thesis that there was a planned and officially enforced policy of cultural op-
pression and psychological destruction of Africans in French speaking African
countries. In our view, the ultimate aim of cultural and psychological subjugation, through education, is political and economic subordination, dependency
and exploitation.

Political independence notwithstanding, modern Africans are still the products of their colonial education. Fundamental changes in education and its
philosophy require mental and intellectual processes and attitudes which have
not yet manifested themselves in post-colonial West African states. It is easily
forgotten that the laws governing political emancipation and educational
emancipation are not the same. While political independence is a necessary
condition for possible changes in the educational system, it is, however, not a
sufficient condition. In his assessment of the general impact of colonial and
post-colonial educational policy on Africans, Jean-Pierre N'Ndiaye observes:

When the new African bourgeoisie glorifies traditional African values, it merely expresses
its sickness for an historical past with which it is breaking without being in a position to
create an autonomous culture. It has adopted the forms of the Western economic bases, an
option which dissociates it from its links with the folk without giving it the opportunity to
have access to the cultural background of the economic group to which it now adheres.
Caught in such a contradiction, the new African elite takes refuge in the valorization of the
African culture in whose economic base it has no longer a share. It takes so much refuge in
it as to become its official defender and protector because it must well give itself an identity.
But, by so doing, the African bourgeoisie claims cultural values that it no longer lives and
feels and from which it is becoming more and more estranged.[19]

Our survey of the French educational philosophy and practices in West
Africa shows the cultural roots of Africa's dependency. What is the picture in
the English-speaking West African states? Apologists of the principles of "Indirect Rule" argue that it guaranteed local cultural autonomy and safeguarded
African traditions and institutions. We reject this view which diverts attention
away from the *real* nature of colonialism. The French instrument of "direct
rule" and the British instrument of "indirect rule" represent different political
and administrative strategies to achieve identical goals: the imposition of
economic and political subjugation on African peoples. The subjugation has
important cultural consequences—the imposition and the spread of British
cultural values and norms in West Africa. Although the French and the British
instruments of political penetration and domination varied, their educational
efforts achieved similar results:

1. The general adoption of the language of the colonial masters as a medium for political, administrative and commercial communication and also for conveying a package of cultural and ideological biases stressing the superiority of the British and the French cultures and civilizations as opposed to what was perceived as "savage" African cultures.
2. The necessity to apply inappropriate pedagogical methods, mainly rote learning, for a variety of subject matters which lack relevance in the child's enviroment.
3. The adoption by Africans of a magical approach to problems facing them in life. In fact, memorizing things outside one's reach directly or indirectly favours verbalism and dilettantism.
4. The general adoption of habits and manners whose rational foundations are alien to African traditions.
5. The naming of all good things produced by Africans themselves after the white man. Foreign domination reached a stage where Africans, whether from the British or French zone of influence, were ashamed to bear African names.

## An Educational Strategy For Cultural Emancipation

There is an urgent need for an educational strategy to overcome cultural alienation and economic dependency in West Africa. Frantz Fanon has lamented the "death of the autochthonous society, cultural lethargy, and petrification of individuals induced by colonialism."[20] If we accept E. Chancele's thesis that "colonization veritably was a social surgery,"[21] then the colonially oppressed are bound to infer that colonialism can never operate without corroding and eroding their social-cultural institutions. Jean-Paul Sartre reminds us that the erosive influence of colonialism begins in childhood: "Hardly had they opened their eyes, do children see their fathers beaten (and maltreated). In psychological terms, they are traumatized."[22] Jean-Paul Sartre continues:

> It is ordered to reduce the inhabitants of the annexed territory to the level of a superior monkey to justify the colonist in his treating them as beasts of burden. The colonial violence does not only assign to itself the aim of making these enslaved people respectful; it also seeks to de-humanize them. Nothing will be spared to liquidate their traditions, to substitute our languages for their own, to destroy their culture without giving them our own; one will brutalize them with fatigue... One aims guns at a peasant; civilians come and impound his land and force him under the effects of the riding-whip to till it for them. If he resists, the soldiers shoot, he is a dead man; if he gives way, he degrades and disgraces himself, he is no longer a man; shame and fear will split his character and disintegrate his person.[23]

We have argued that the processes that supported the domination of West Africa by the Europeans did not end on the very day West African countries achieved political independence. Their "suppressed rage," Jean-Paul Sartre reminds us, "for having failed to explode, reproduces itself and destroys the oppressed people themselves."[24] The development policies being implemented in West Africa and the philosophy underlying them clearly indicate that despite political independence, cultural autonomy is still far from our reach. This manifests itself in the uncritical pursuit and application of what is called "international standard," which is now largely responsible for the growing foreign cultural influence and economic exploitation of Africa. An educational philosophy which is capable of redeeming Africa from dependency must be based on the premise that "There is no neutral education. Education is either for domestication or for freedom. Although it is customarily conceived as a conditioning process, education can equally be redirected to become an instrument for deconditioning. An initial choice is (therefore) required of the educator."[25] Colonial education or its immediate successor, post-colonial education, cannot be neutral in an African environment. Education must necessarily aim at producing a type of man and a type of intellectual environment that unconditionally favours and supports that type of man. This requires, in Paulo Freire's view, a growing historical awareness of oneself in a larger international political context, and Africa's role in a colonial world had been limited and subservient.[26] Fundamental changes in education are not likely to occur in the absence of important changes in the international system and in the internal socio-economic and socio-political order of African countries themselves. In other words, a strong two-dimensional shock is necessary for Africans to establish educational systems which are meant to serve their self-interests. As Frantz Fanon once observed with reference to the black people of the Antilles,[27] without such a shock, a positive education will be extremely difficult to achieve and our educational system will continue to be passive, accommodating, and adaptive to colonial interests.

Assuming that all the major psychological and political conditions for educational change can be fulfilled, one other important task is to define the type of man we want our educational system to produce. Paulo Freire reminds us that "Every educational practice implies a (suitable and workable) concept of man and the world."[28] The philosophy of education and educational programmes derived from this thesis must establish a dialectical functional link between man and his immediate environment as well as his historical conditions of life. We reject an educational system whose products specialize in exploitation or perpetuate the present social order in which a small class exploits and dominates the majority. The guiding principles of an educational system capable of transforming the colonial order should emphasize thought, language and dialogue as strategic instruments for the eradication of intellectual dependency.

Language can be an instrument of cultural emancipation and also an instrument of domination. The language of the colonial masters serves the latter purpose. French and English, like other languages, are not just neutral means of disseminating technically objective knowledge. They are media through which the French and the English express their positive feelings and preferences and project stereotypes about their colonial subjects and other outgroups. Languages can and have been manipulated to serve specific economic and political objectives. English and French have historically served to articulate, defend and sell to Africans the cultural baggage of Europe. These languages cannot serve Africa's interest, which is political and cultural emancipation. The use of alien languages to express views about African existential conditions not only distorts African realities and diverts attention from what gives a sense to them but it prevents Africans from having a fair and reliable information on the same realities. Education demands that the language of its instruction be fully accessible to its students and be rooted in their cultural, ideological and political environment.

Besides the language of instruction, another important issue in educational policy for West Africa is whether to give priority to educational qualification or the quality of education. Very often educational qualification has been equated with the quality of education, an educational philosophy which contradicts the objective conditions in post-colonial societies. By saying that "...it is difficult to determine with precision the elements that constitute the quality of education,"[29] Correa not only justifies the synonymous use of the two concepts but draws attention to possible divergences between educational qualification and the quality of education. We should note that both terms cannot be used synonymously. Educational qualification mainly describes and emphasizes the way one goes through the educational system and the level of performance achieved. Whether the courses taken are relevant to a given social-cultural environment is another thing. On the other hand, the quality of education refers basically to the intrinsic value of education, to the effective contribution of education in emancipating human beings from the objective constraints put before man by his environment. A reform-oriented education programme should ensure that educational qualification does not overshadow the need for the quality of education.

Our educational philosophy and practice, both the colonial and post-colonial, are qualification-biased; and as a result, both are largely opposed to our concept of the quality of education. The reason for this seems to lie in the strong but naive belief in the universality of Western technologies and methods. Since technology emerges as a result of the dialectical interactions of man with his particular environment, one must conclude that its effects, which are never neutral, must be relative. An educational system that is built on the idea of universal technology is bound to foster technological dependency. The frame of reference and orientation of an educational system whose goal is human emancipation must be locally rather than internationally rooted. Such education should be guided by the following insights from Paulo Freire.

No single educational action can afford to get rid either of a reflexion on man or of an analysis of the conditions of his cultural milieu. There is no education outside human societies; there are no human beings in the vacuum. Man is a being with temporal and spatial roots. From thence is he situated and dated. The instrumentality of education—something fundamentally more than the simple training of technical cadres in accordance with the developmental vocation of a country—depends on the harmony obtained between the ontological vocation of this being situated and dated and the particular conditions of his environment. Education is only a valid and valuable instrument (of emancipation) if it interacts dialectically with the context of the society to which it applies.[30]

The basic issues for an educational policy designed to liberate people from their state of dependency deal with the concept of man, his role in a special historical context, and the right perspective on which to base educational work. Education can be centrifugally or centripetally oriented. The contemporary West African educational system is centrifugally oriented, based as it is on foreign philosophies and foreign know-how. A centripetally oriented education is based on local realities and directs its intellectual efforts towards the achievement of cultural freedom. Educational problems caused by dependency can largely find their solution in a countervailing educational strategy which we call a centripetal approach to education.

## BIBLIOGRAPHY

BALANDIER, GEORGE. *Sociologie Actuelle de l'Afrique Noire.* Paris, 1963.
CAUTINHO, JOAO DA VEIGA. "Preface" to Freire, Paulo. *Cultural Action for Freedom.* London: Harmondsworth, 1977.
CORREA, H. *The Economics of Human Resources: Contributions to Economic Analysis.* Amsterdam, 1963.
EMGE, RICHARD MARTINUS. *Auswaertige Kulturpolitik: Eine soziologische Analyse einiger ihrer Funktionen, Bedingungen und Formen.* Berlin, 1967.
FANON, FRANTZ. *Pour la Revolution Africaine.* Paris, 1969.
———. *Les Damnes de la Terre.* Paris, 1961.
MASPERO, FRANCOIS. *L'Ecole Emancipee: La Repression dans l'Enseignement.* Paris, 1972.
MEISTER, ALBERT. *L'Afrique peut-elle partir: Changement Social et Developpement en Afrique Orientale.* Paris, 1966.
MOUMOUNI, ABDOU. *L'Education en Afrique.* Paris, 1967.
MYRDAL, GUNNAR. *Une Economie Internationale.* Paris, 1958.
N'NDIAYE, JEAN-PIERRE. *Elites Africaines et Culture Occidentale—Assimilation ou Resistance?* Paris, 1969.
SARTRE, JEAN-PAUL. "Introduction" to Fanon, Frantz. *Les Damnes de la Terre.* Paris, 1961.
VON DIAS, PATRICK. *Kritische Ueberlegungen zur internationalen Strategie der Bildungshilfe.* Deutsche Stiftung fuer Entwicklungs-laender, Entwicklung und Zusammenarbeit. 1970.
VON RECUM, HASSO. "Bildungsplanung in Entwicklungslaendern." (Dokumentation). *Staendige Konferenz der Kultusminister der Laender in der Bundesrepublik Deutschland.* No. 9. Frankfort on the Main, December 1963.
WEBER, MAX. "Politik als Beruf." *Gesammelte politische Schriften.* Munich, 1921.

## NOTES

1 Patrick von Dias, *Kritische Ueberlegungen zur internationalen Strategie der Bildungshilfe* Deutsche Stiftung fuer Entwicklungs-laender (Entwicklung und Zusammenarbeit, P/1/6/7/70), p. 6.
2 Hasso von Recum, *Bildungsplanung in Entwicklungslaendern,* Dokumentation, Staendige Konferenz der Kultusminster der Laender in der Bundesrepublik Deutschland (Frankfort on the Main, December 1963), p. 22.
3 Richard Martinus Emge, *Auswaertige Kulturpolitik: Ein soziologische Analyse einiger ihrer Funktionen, Bedingungen und Formen* (Berlin, 1967), pp. 37-40.
4 Ibid., p. 39.
5 Max Weber, "Politik als Beruf," *Gesammelte politische Schriften* (Munich, 1921), p. 397.

6 Emge, p. 110.
7 Arnold Toynbee quoted in Albert Meister, *L'Afrique peut-elle partir? Changement Social et Developpement en Afrique Orientale* (Paris, 1966), p. 58, n. 1.
8 Jacob Viner, "The Role of the United States in the World Economy," cited in Gunnar Myrdal, *Une Economie Internationale* (Paris, 1958), p. 175.
9 Maurice Delafosse quoted in Abdou Moumouni, *L'Education en Afrique* (Paris, 1967), p. 45.
10 Abdou Moumouni, *L'Education en Afrique* (Paris, 1967), p. 47. [Editor: The educational policies and experiences discussed by the author are drawn from the practices which prevailed in French-speaking West Africa. They apply, by extension, to English-speaking areas.]
11 M. Brevie quoted in Moumouni, p. 54.
12 Ibid.
13 Roume quoted in Moumouni, p. 60.
14 Ibid.
15 Moumouni, p. 55 [Editor: The Decree of 1924 deals with education in French West Africa.]
16 Roume, p. 56.
17 Moumouni, p. 55.
18 Roume, quoted in Moumouni, p. 57.
19 Jean-Pierre N'Ndiaye, *Elites Africaines et Culture Occidentale—Assimilation ou Resistance?* (Paris, 1969), p. 9.
20 Frantz Fanon, *Les Damnes de la Terre* (Paris, 1961), p. 69.
21 E. Chancele, "La Question Coloniale," Quoted in Georges Balandier, *Sociologie Actuelle de l'Afrique Noire* (Paris, 1963), p. 3.
22 Jean-Paul Sartre, Introduction to Frantz Fanon, *Les Damnes de la Terre* (Paris, 1961), p. 16.
23 Ibid., p. 15.
24 Ibid., p. 17.
25 Joao da Veiga Cautinho, Preface to Paulo Freire, *Cultural Action for Freedom* (London: Harmondsworth, 1977), p. 9.
26 Paulo Freire, *Cultural Action for Freedom* (London: Harmondsworth, 1977), pp. 14-17; See also Francois Maspero, "L'Ecole Emancipee," in *La Repression dans l'Enseignement* (Paris, 1972).
27 Frantz Fanon, *Pour la Revolution Africaine* (Paris, 1969), p. 22.
28 Freire, p. 21.
29 H. Correa, *The Economics of Human Resources: Contributions or Economic Analysis* (Amsterdam, 1963), p. 89.
30 Freire, *Cultural Action for Freedom*, 1977.

# Dependency Theory:
# Problems of Cultural Autonomy
# and Cultural Convergence

VICTOR C. UCHENDU

*University of Illinois, Urbana-Champaign, U.S.A.*

*The Truth Is The Whole* (Hegel)

WHEN MAJOR SOCIAL ISSUES fall into the hands of academic social scientists, they not only assume a life of their own but become unusually endowed with a great survival capacity. This is probably why generations of philosophers, social scientists and theorists regularly plough back into old problems, pose new questions and propose new answers about them, often from the perspectives of their own time.

Times have changed and traditional answers are no longer good enough for old problems. The changing times have forced on the modern world two contradictory developments. The first in the gross inequality in income and wealth among nations. We have the paradoxical growth of the "poverty of nations" at a period in human history when the wealth of the world is unprecedented. The second development is the growing institutional, and in some places, cultural interdependence among the nations of the world which creates the second paradox—a growing world cultural convergence at the period when cultural autonomy for the nation state is pursued as an explicit political goal.

This paper links both developments. It employs the theory of cultural dynamics to examine both the limits of dependency theory and the claims of cultural autonomy and cultural convergence.

Dependency theory and the theory of cultural convergence, each has its apologists and high priests. My function here is not to please either but to enlighten both. My task, which is undertaken with the understanding that final answers and explanations may not be found, is based on the proposition that new answers and explanations must, nevertheless, be pursued. The structure of the paper is simple. It presents a summary of the dependency theory as well as the elements of cultural theory that will be employed in our analysis; then the theory of cultural convergence is presented and its claims are analysed against those of dependency theory. Briefly stated, the cultural content of dependency theory is the subject of this paper.

## Basis for Development Theory

A central problem of our time—and in fact of all times—is the poverty of nations. Poverty is not new in history. What is new is the political rejection of the coexistence of gross disparity in income and wealth, both within and among nations. Our traditional ideas and theories about the origin of poverty have undergone a radical change. Poverty is no longer accepted as the result of individual failure; and the view that it is caused by race or geography has been rightly discredited. There is an alternative proposition that accounts for the poverty of individuals by the way their society is organized—a forerunner to the thesis that the poverty of nations is caused by past and continuing exploitation by the world dominant economic system. This thesis is at the heart of dependency theory.

When in 1776, Adam Smith wrote magisterially on the ways of increasing the wealth of nations, he was addressing a mercantilist rather than an industrial or post-industrial world. The world is different in the 1970s. It is no longer the "wealth of nations" but the "poverty of nations" that calls for an explanation. The paradox is that the world is not poor, in wealth or in income; but most of the nations and most of the peoples of the world are materially poor; and increasingly they reject and resent their poverty. This situation has called for a re-evaluation of orthodox economic theories and development paradigms.

An influential development paradigm, as much abused as it is used, is that by Walt W. Rostow, an economic historian. In his very broad conception of world economic history, Rostow[1] assigns to the post-traditional societies the attributes of economic underdevelopment. For Rostow, the pre-Newtonian world as well as many post-Newtonian societies are pre-modern or traditional societies because they "developed within limited production functions which put a ceiling on the level of attainable output per head."[2] In this view, Rostow conceives economic development, and in fact, modern societal transformation, as beginning in Western Europe about the late seventeenth and early eighteenth centuries when Europeans, led by Britain, started to apply regularly and systematically their achievements in science and technology to agriculture and industry.

Rostow devotes four of his five-stage growth theory to the elaboration of the processes—both socio-cultural and institutional—which result in self-generating development. His transitional societies, which face the preconditions for take-off—and Nigeria comes to mind—must create their own development institutions and infrastructure, generate science-based knowledge and apply this knowledge to production. To achieve a "take-off," which will lead eventually to the last two stages—"the drive to maturity" and the state of "high mass-consumption"—resistances to steady growth and development must be broken. This requires the directive force and powers of a politically effective national state. In Rostow's words, the "take-off" awaits

...not only the building up of social overhead capital and a surge of technological development in industry and agriculture, but also the emergence to political power of a group prepared to regard the modernization of the economy as serious, high-order political business.[3]

Development in post-independence Africa appears, from the pronouncements of Africa's political leaders, a high-order political business. It is also a complex business, in fact, a more complex business than what Britain or United States had to face in their time. The complex interaction between the nation-state and modernity on the one hand, and the aspirations and philosophies developed by African leaders in their struggles against colonial rule on the other, make African development an essentially political exercise. In Africa, as in many new nation-states, development implies a dual responsibility: the political and cultural management of a plural society and the building of a political economy, sometimes on a new basis. This requires a delicate balancing of economic resources and political forces—an exercise that sometimes sacrifices efficiency and economy. For a continent whose resources are unevenly distributed by nature—a maldistribution which man, through bad policy, has worsened—the inefficient use of the limited resources has tended to penalize both political and economic progress.

The dimensions of African poverty and underdevelopment were not fully appreciated during the colonial struggles; and few still understand and much less appreciate the difficulties of transforming a poor, post-colonial economy into a prosperous one. When Kwame Nkrumah admonished Africans to "Seek ye the political kingdom and all the rest will be added unto you," his prayer was a prescriptive doctrine of political economy which all African leaders considered a necessary and sufficient condition for development.

The decade of the sixties—Africa's independence decade—coincided with the United Nation's first Development Decade. We discovered in this decade that our economic calculations were wrong; and that political independence—and some doubt how independent we are—is not a sufficient condition for achieving our economic, social and political objectives. The vast majority of our people remain impoverished. If social development means improved housing, two good meals a day, clean water supplies and ability to send our children to school at the cost we can afford, we have not yet begun. When you add Africa's capacity to build new slums in her cities, our inability to produce the essential foods we need, and our capacity to misgovern ourselves and our economies, you have summarized the contents of Rene Dumont's treatise on the subject, *False Start in Africa.*[4]

Africa's mines and export-oriented agriculture still feed the industrial machines and factories of Europe, America, and increasingly, Japan. We still import most of our manufactured goods, mainly consumed by some 5-10 percent of our population who get from 50-70 percent of the continent's cash income. Nigeria probably has a better income spread, thanks to the booming oil sector and the political will of the present governing elite, but the continent presents a picture of growing disparity in income, opportunities and life chances.

In attempts to explain Africa's underdevelopment, orthodox economic theorists seem to have run out of paradigms. From Ragner Nurske's vicious circle thesis in which, "...a country is poor because it is poor," we entered Leibenstein's "quasi stable equilibrium" thesis in which an unspecified minimum per capita income level has to be created in order to generate sustained internal growth.

Economic achievements through our agricultural sector provided a stimulus to other varieties of growth theories. It has been observed and confirmed that Africans are not the tradition-bound peasants of development literature. That on the contrary, they are aggressive, petty entrepreneurs, able and willing to exploit new economic opportunities, if their governments would let them, and if the necessary institutional infrastructure can be established. The Ghanaian agricultural experience, where small holder migrant farmers, later joined by many others, pioneered and established 2.25 million hectares of cocoa land, with a minimum of technical and financial assistance from the colonial government and institutions, is a classic example. This and many others, including examples of Nigeria's cocoa and rubber fields, lent credibility to the "vent for surplus" model of development in which agriculture became the essential engine for growth. Diffusion of innovation studies and processes of modernization were part of ths package.

By the mid 1960s Africa's development strategy assumed a bimodal path. State farms, group farms and settlement farms were created and supported in many countries, often at the expense of the large but unorganized small holder agricultural sector. This was the age of tractors and tractorization. In many African countries of the mid 1960s, agricultural production for domestic markets fell as the supply of farm tractors rose. Prices of foodstuffs rose and the bills from food imports multiplied. The products of substitution industries—where they are not starved to death, as in Ghana, because of foreign exchange bottlenecks—become too expensive for the prevailing purchasing power in the domestic economy.

Persistent underdevelopment, the picture of which has been presented, had been explained by Boeke as the result of a clash of two contradictory cultures and political economies, consisting of a foreign dominant industrial system and a domestic subservient economic system. With typical colonial arrogance, Boeke attributes to the industrial system, in this case Dutch in origin, a superior culture, and to the dominated system, an inferior culture. He argued that the Dutch colonial, capitalist system required its own "philosophy of life, an attitude towards life" both of which are radically different from and therefore clash with, the attitudes of colonially dominated peoples, whose "social bonds" he described as "original and organic."[5] Boeke's thesis inspired structural dualism. Although certain aspects of Boeke's thesis have empirical support, his extreme cultural arguments alienated a number of people. Dualism has a great descriptive power. The most casual visitor to our continent will be struck by the contrasts between Africa's airports and Government Reservation Areas (GRA) on the one hand and our rural areas, on the other. But dualistic theories still lack explanatory power. They fail to explain the origin and the dynamics of a system or a situation which is, on the surface, dichotomous, but in reality a unified whole.[6]

## Dependency Thesis: A Summary

The search for adequate theories of social development has completed a circle. Interest in grand, all-embracing theories of social development characteristic of the nineteenth century gave way to intermediate theories in the twentieth century, but interest in the development or lack of development in Third World countries has revived holistic theories of which the dependency theory is an important example.

The paternity of dependency theory is not contested. Although it has attracted a large number of adherents, its genealogy is shallow. Dependency theory arose as a radical criticism of conventional economic policies and the orthodox economic theories that inspired them. Andre Gunder Frank, a prolific writer on the subject of dependency, is the undisputed founder of the new school. Other seminal thinkers on the subject include Celso Furtado, Henrique Cardoso, Theotonio Dos Santos, A. Emmanuel, Samir Amin, Paul Baran and P. Sweezy.

The most polemic application of dependency theory to African experience comes from Walter Rodney's *How Europe Underdeveloped Africa.*[7] Rodney's study contrasts with George Beckford's *Persistent Poverty,*[8] a study of plantation economies in the West Indies, in both rhetoric and clear attention to evidence.

Dependent theory aspires to restore the unity of the social sciences which extreme disciplinary specialization by scholars and departmentalization by universities seem to have eroded. Samir Amin addresses this question when he criticizes the weakness of individual social science disciplines:

> Conventional Sociology having developed as a reply to historical materialism, has the same bourgeois ideological foundation and seeks to justify the established order by demonstrating "universal" harmonies. Political Science wavers between journalism and formalism. Geographers are content to juxtapose facts—ignoring the basic question for geographers—how natural conditions act upon social formations. History continues to be anecdotal in character: if history cannot be everything, it is nothing.[9]

The social sciences do not want to be nothing. Dependency theory provides them an opportunity to be something. Social scientists can, and should cooperate and pool their energies to help achieve self-sustaining growth and development in post colonial societies.

What actually is dependence? Theotonio Dos Santos attempts an answer. He defines dependence as "a situation in which the economy of certain countries is conditioned by the development and expansion of another economy to which the former is subjected."[10] In Santos' view, the relation of interdependence can only be dialectical; the relation between two or more economies or systems must be such that one assumes dominance, decides its fate as well as the fate of others. He distinguished three forms of dependence:

1. Colonial dependence, which is marked by export trade, mainly agriculture and mineral products from the colonies; and the import of manufactured products from the colonizing power.
2. Financial-industrial dependence which, in the African development experience, creates enclave economies, and gives birth to "growth without development."
3. Technological dependence, a post-World War II development that coincided with the rise of Multi-national Corporations, which have enormous venture capital, and are able and willing to invest in dependent economies but unwilling to surrender decision making or let out technical secrets to manufacturers.

It is Santos' argument that as industrialization proceeds in a dependent economy, technological and other forms of dependence deepen. He suggests three reasons for this development.[11] First, industrial development depends initially on the export sector to earn the necessary foreign exchange; and in developing African countries, the export earnings have come from agriculture or mining, and in a few countries, from both. This linkage between export trade and industrialization has tended to preserve the export sector from rapid policy shifts, and many African countries have achieved export capacity at the expense of their domestic food requirements, including the development of the internal market. Where the traditional export sector is foreign dominated, the remittance of profits abroad from that sector further limits internal demand, thus creating the classic case of growth without development.

Second, industrial development is strongly conditioned by fluctuations in balance of payments. This creates deficits in three areas: trade relations; capital accounts due to repatriation of huge profits etc.; and in two forms of foreign financing—to cover existing deficits and to finance development loans.

Third, industrialization requires importation of machinery and raw materials which must be paid for in hard currencies.

Dependency theory is a version of structural theory applied to the political economy. The utility of structuralism is that it can be applied to any conceivable phenomenon. Anthropologists have applied it successfully to kinship and symbolic studies. In the context of the Nigerian economy, Okonjo[12] used it as a frame for his inaugural lecture. And in development literature, it is gaining ascendancy.

The most provocative application of structuralism to a major contemporary problem, that of imperialism, is by Johan Galtung.[13] Galtung conceives the world as consisting of Centre (C) and Periphery (P) nations. Each has a centre (c) and a periphery (p). There is a high degree of verticality between Centre and Periphery nations in terms of power, privilege and division of labour. Centre nations exercise power. They have autonomy, which means power "over self" and the ability to set their own goals. They exercise power over the Periphery nations, whose goals they tend to set; and what is more important is their ability to get the Periphery nations to pursue these goals, which they come to accept, as in their national interest. In the power game, the Centre nations exercise the three aspects of structural power—exploitation, fragmentation and penetration.

In the content of relations between the Centre and Periphery nations, Galtung postulates three dyadic structures—two of which are harmonious and one disharmonious.

1. There is a harmony of interest between the centre in the Centre nation and the centre in the Periphery nation, implying that the elites of the two nations have common interests and also protect each other.
2. There is more disharmony of interest within the Periphery nation than within the Centre nation, implying that the wealth of the elite in the Periphery is not legitimized. In the new Marxist idiom, the battle ground has shifted from the old industrial societies to poor countries.
3. There is disharmony of interest between the periphery in the Centre nation and the periphery in the Periphery nation—a thesis that does not give comfort to the theory of a world class system.

Structuralism can lay claim to have provided dependency theory a new set of terminology, which of course has been enriched by contact with and stimulus from Marxist economics. But the shift in focus, from national to regional and now to global history, is essentially the original contribution from dependency theory.

What are the claims of dependency theory? The theory may be summarized in a number of propositions.

1. Underdevelopment results from dependence. According to Gunder Frank, underdevelopment in Latin America and elsewhere, developed as the result of the colonial structure of world capitalist development. The new developed countries were *never* underdeveloped, though they may have been undeveloped. In contrast to the development of the world metropolis which is no one's satellite, the development of the national and other subordinate metropoles is limited by their satellite status.[14]
2. Underdevelopment results mainly from exploitation of the weak by the strong. In Frank's classic phrase, "Centres of intercourse are also centres of exploitation."[15] Rodney re-echoes the same theme: "All of the countries named as underdeveloped in the world are exploited by others and the underdevelopment with which the world is now preoccupied is a product of capitalist, imperialist, and colonialist exploitation."[16]
3. Development and underdevelopment have a dialectical relationship, the former impoverishes the latter while the latter enriches the former. On this dialectical relationship, Rodney observes "...the two help produce each other by interaction. Western Europe and Africa had a relationship which ensured the transfer of wealth from Africa to Europe."[17] Samir Amin devotes much of his *Unequal Development* to this proposi-

tion. He reaffirms the unity and indivisibility of the world capitalist economy when he writes:

> The predominance of the capitalist mode of production is also expressed on another plane. It constitutes a world system in which all the formations, central and peripheral alike, are arranged in a single system, organic and hierarchical. Thus there are not two world markets, the capitalist and socialist, but only one, the capitalist world market, in which Eastern Europe participates marginally.[18]

It is the structure of this single world market system that dependency theory views in terms of core-periphery image, an image linked with dependency. Wallerstein supports this unitary theory of the capitalist world market, arguing that even in the sixteenth century, the core and the periphery of the world economy were not two separate economies. At that time, as now, the same economic laws governed the world economy, but the periphery and the core systems, then as now, were assigned different functions, the basis for differential rewards and therefore, exploitation.[19]

Given the image of the world economy as a single system, dependency theorists have tended to reject the dualistic thesis of Boeke and its later reinterpretations and formulations. Frank was blunt on the matter, "Dual society thesis is false and the policy recommendations (based on it will) serve only to intensify and perpetuate the very conditions of underdevelopment they are supposedly designed to remedy."[20]

4. Underdevelopment is not just the product of local or national history; it is the product of a global, imperial history. Frank argues that "contemporary underdevelopment is in large part the historical product of past and continuing economic, and other relations between the satellite, underdeveloped and the now developed metropolitan countries."[21] It is Rodney's argument that Africa was in the process of developing vibrant, cultural, economic and political systems when its growth was halted, and even reversed by the incursion and activities of European colonial powers. The view that the evolution of the world economy moves as a whole; and its achievements and fortunes unequally shared between dependent countries and the dominant industrial powers, is a persuasive one indeed.

5. Underdevelopment is not caused by archaic social structure and traditional institutional arrangements. This is the basis on which dependency theorists reject modernization and innovation theories. This position is not surprising for a theory that attributes underdevelopment *entirely* to external exploitation and sees internal exploitation as nothing but the extension of the former. In his very combative language, Frank declares:

> Underdevelopment is not due to the survival of archaic institutions and the existence of capital shortage in regions that have remained isolated from the stream of world history. On the contrary, underdevelopment was and still is generated by the very historical process which also generated economic development: the development of capitalism itself.[22]

The view that traditional social structure, particularly in Latin America, can be absolved from the region's underdevelopment flies in the face of all available ethnography in the area. It appears that Frank has taken Baran and Sweezy's statement too literally, when they advised: "In a very real sense the function of both science and art is to exaggerate, provided what is exaggerated is truth and not falsehood."[23] I am afraid that truth that is worth the name needs no adornment. The subtle difference between the liberty of the artist and the responsibility of the scientist is compromised when scientific truths are adorned. Scientists may not avoid all margins of error, but unlike the artist, they are not allowed to build in error into their findings, even for the shock effect.

6. De-satellization is the only cure to underdevelopment. This makes dependency theory a prescriptive theory. Rodney states the reason, in the African context: "African development is possible only on the basis of a radical break with the international capitalist system which has been the principal agency of underdevelopment in Africa over the last five centuries."[24] The policy of self-reliance seems to support this prescription. But self-reliance must have some basis, some local resource to rely on. Guinea tried it and collapsed after a few years. When one realizes that of the 25 hard core, poor countries listed by the United Nations, 16 are in Africa, 8 in Asia and Oceania, and only one, Haiti, in Latin America, then the thin basis on which Africa's self-reliance strategy is built becomes apparent.

The chief argument in support of the de-satellization thesis is that international involvements lead to exploitation. Studies of the Multinational corporations show them as *the* new form of economic imperialism dedicated to the proposition that the *Global Reach* spells global profits; and global profits imply global power—power to control three fundamental resources of economic life: the technology of production; finance capital; and marketing.[25]

## Dependency Thesis: An Assessment

Although dependency theory is anti-West in tone and pro-Marxist in terminology, the central message of the theory must be equally disturbing to both the ideologues and apologists of capitalism and socialism alike. While it is a call against international capitalism, it is not a call for international socialism. It is a strong argument for the independence of the Third World countries. The selective use and abuse of economic history by dependence theorists has been ably dealt with by Hopkins,[26] whose many important insights I share.

It is not quite clear when African economies or polities were really independent, in terms of the dependency theory. Hopkins asks: "...what might be termed pre-dependence period" in Africa? I wonder how we handle inter-African interactions that resulted in unequal benefits and in internal colonialism. What do we know of pre-dependence African political economies? What were their central emphases? Why is it that in many African traditional states, the traditional economies lagged very much behind their sophisticated political cultures?[27] What are the implications of these traditional economies for the dependency theory?

In the context of this paper, how valid is the claim that economic dependency necessarily leads to the status of a *dependent* or an *inferior* culture? Does the world capitalist system which generates underdevelopment for Third World countries also generate Little cultural traditions for them while retaining the Great cultural traditions?

Dependency theory has stimulated a lot of interest in the theory of unequal exchange. The major emphasis has been on international trade and the distribution of the benefits of technology. We must redirect attention to cultural exchange, using the theory of cultural dynamics to investigate the impact of the world economic system on national cultures.

## Dependency Theory and Cultural Dynamics

Dependency theorists have not paid much attention to the implications of their theory on culture. Is a dependent economy or polity also a dependent culture? If the answer is positive, what are the attributes of a dependent culture? How do we reconcile the concept of a dependent culture with that of a convergent culture? To answer these questions, we will draw from the findings of cultural dynamics and exchange theory, but, as a preliminary, we must examine those aspects of the concepts of culture which are relevant to our discourse.

## The Notion of Culture

By culture we mean the man-made part of the environment including the ideas and symbols we use. The material environment is the basis for objective culture; and the way man-made part of the environment is perceived constitutes the *subjective* culture. Different social-cultural environments provide individuals and societies with different schedules of reinforcement which help them develop distinct points of view about the way the environment is structured.[28] For example, some societies have accepted that socialism is the surest way to development and some think it is capitalism; while others think that the essential features of both systems can and should be combined.

There is no such thing as a human nature independent of culture. "We are incomplete or unfinished animals who complete or finish ourselves through culture."[29] But we are enculturated through particular forms of a culture that make us Nigerians, Ghanaians or Africans. In a recent statement on the subject, I have argued, following the insights of Van Peursen, that

> Culture is more than just a heritage, an historical product: it is more than the expression of man's mode of living, something that individuals in each society must undergo as a kind of fate or *rites de passage*. That...culture must be seen as an instrumental agent, as another mode of intervention in our social and economic life.[30]

There is also a *semiotic* view of culture that draws from the seminal ideas of Max Weber. Weber believes that man is an animal suspended in "webs of significance" which he himself has spun. We take culture to be those webs. In this context, the analysis of culture becomes less an experimental science in search of laws but more an interpretative one in search of meaning. In the context of the theory of dependency, the task of cultural theory is to seek the meaning of dependency from the *nomethetic* or normative dimension as well as the *idiographic* or personal dimension.

Elaborating on Weber's views, and following a line of thought stretching back at least to Vico, Parsons[31] views culture as a system of symbols by which man confers meaning or significance upon his own experience. To illustrate from the theme of this workshop, a dependent status is more likely to arouse emotion among the exploited than among the exploiters; and among those in dependent status who perceive the fact of their exploitation than those who do not. These differences may reflect differences in symbolic communication. Symbol systems, which are man-made, are not only shared, conventional, ordered and learned, but they provide human beings with a meaningful framework for orienting and relating themselves to one another, to the world around them, and to themselves. They are at once a product and a determinant of social interaction. They are an important information or cybernetic system.

## Cultural Dynamics

Rapid change is a striking characteristic of modern society. The growing demand of modern society makes rapid, cultural change inevitable. It also has widened the concept of culture, making the notion of culture as an interventionist agent increasingly popular.

The very idea of culture implies change—adaptation and readaptation of forms, institutions and ideas and their application to changing situations. Culture change as a dynamic process implies among other things, choice-making in society. The four major factors that induce new choice-making in society are:

(a) the changing relationships with the environment
(b) new ideas and innovations
(c) powerful drives to progress which compel the eradication of observable social ills
(d) natural inclinations to compare and evaluate social achievements which induce imitation

In the context of dependency theory, the forces at work are (*a*), (*c*) and (*d*). As we have seen, the relationship between the Third World countries and the developed countries is one of institutional dominance of the former by the latter; and there is some effort by the Third World to reduce this gross imbalance, a process that involves continuing assessment and reassessment of comparative achievements or lack of achievements and reasons for them.

Choice-making, whether by organized society or by individuals, is the basis of cultural change. In the cultural domain, choice-making is no longer a simple affair. It is not even a uniform process. The unevenness in choice-making in society leads, inevitably, to cultural variations. In many West African societies, cultural variations flow from at least three sources: cultural specialization; competitive accentuation of social, economic and political differences; and differential enculturation. Of the three sources of cultural variations, the competitive accentuation of differences is most congruent with the strategy of independent development. The two other forces are dependent on it.

In process analysis of culture, distinctions are made between recurrent processes and directional processes. Recurrent processes are short run events which occur in micro-time scales. The emphasis in recurrent processes is upon repetitiveness of the pattern. The domestic cycle is a good illustration: individuals are born into the family, are socialized by society and later they die and their roles are reallocated to successors. Directional processes, on the other hand, occur in macro-time scales and involve cumulative shifts in structures of social and cultural systems. It is clear that the development prescription from dependency theory will lead to a *directional* rather than *recurrent* type of change. Directional change—in cultural or social system—is generated by tension; and inequality whether it is cultural, economic, political or institutional is a major factor in directional change.

We may hypothesize that the value-choices made by a society in the course of its history or which are imposed upon it from outside will dictate whether the course of change will be directional or recurrent. Following this hypothesis, it may be predicted that where the basic value system of a society calls for *incorporation* of borrowed or foreign elements into its culture, the dynamics of change will tend to be recurrent rather than directional; and where the principle of cultural integration emphasizes either *elaboration* or *pattern saturation*, the dynamic of change will tend to be directional. If there is strong evidence that Third World countries are more interested in cultural elaboration and pattern saturation than in cultural incorporation, then it appears that the Marxist revisionists who predict social revolution in poor countries rather than in established industrial societies, may be supported by evidence from cultural analysis.

## Cultural Convergence

The world may be divided by the harsh realities of social and economic inequality and the memory of past, and in places, continuing exploitation and injustice. Equally true, the world is more interdependent in the 1970s than in any period in man's recent history. Cultural convergence is, therefore, a fact of our emergent history.

What is cultural convergence? According to Peter Wiles,[32] the origin of "convergence" in social analysis is obscure. In political analysis, the convergence thesis has a strong Cold War association. During the Cold War, the ideology of Yugoslavia's foreign policy assumed an explicitly convergent thesis; and in this sense, the primacy of conception rather than of use must go to the Titoists.

The early advocates of the convergence theory were all political optimists. They expected the behaviour of the United States and the Soviet Union to change in a way that would lead to a "meeting of the minds" on fundamental international issues. Three reasons were given in support of the theory.[33]

The first argument was that new rational methods of economic planning must eventually supercede both the free market of the capitalist West and the command system of *a priori* allocations by the East.

Second, that reason must eventually triumph over dogma, or managers over ideologues so that the policies of the Soviet leadership would become more tolerant.

Third, that rich societies that enjoy a high level of mass consumption all tend to be at least tolerant, if not similar.

The general tone of the theory of political convergence is that, if only the U.S.A. and the U.S.S.R. can avoid annihilating each other and humanity, they will over time, grow so similar or at least so reasonable that hatred between them might turn into coesixtence. Commenting on the first thesis, Peter Wiles makes the point that, "If dissimilarity is a sure cause of enmity, similarity is not a sure cure."[34] The convergent thesis has other implications which might undermine the political and cultural autonomy of nation-states but would preserve the capitalist and socialist systems as long as their behaviour becomes mutually tolerant. The implications may be restated in the form of two propositions. First, Western Europe and their present satellite countries in the Third World that remain capitalist, will reproduce the Euro-American development pattern. Second, Eastern European socialist countries and the Third World countries aspiring to be socialists, will eventually reproduce the historical stages of U.S.S.R.

Do the advances in sciences, technology and management support the thesis that the prevailing method of resource allocation may be superceded? Contrary to prevailing folklore, economic rationality is a basic problem to all economic systems, no matter their ideological basis or cultural level. In economics, the word 'rational' implies that resources must be so allocated as to maximize outputs, and these outputs be so chosen as to maximize consumer satisfaction. But in the broader socio-cultural sense this preoccupation with economic rationality may be "irrational" in that a delicately optimal adjustment of resource allocation is not an end in itself but a means, "one way among many to economic prosperity," and a way quite likely to conflict with others such as a "more just distribution of income."[35] In trying to balance the demands of economic rationality with the requirements of social justice, socialist economies use arbitrary allocation systems and capitalist economies use the free, but now heavily regulated, market system. The revolution in linear programming techniques, mathematics, and the rise of the computer are rendering both free market and the arbitrary allocations system obsolete. "The introduction of [linear programming and other sophisticated planning techniques] into the Soviet Union has shaken the Marxist theory of value to its base. Instead of labour alone, land and capital also must receive prices; scarcity is recognized as central to value; the margin and not the average is the crucial magnitude."[36]

The managerial revolution, a product of bureaucratism, is the real common denominator between the East and the West arising from the growing demand for reasonableness, expertise and disinterestedness that characterize all complex systems. For instance, the trained manager has tended to usurp some of the roles of the shareholder in the West as he has usurped the roles of the Workers' Council in Yugoslavia and the Party Boss in the U.S.S.R. In the new nation-states, the successors to the colonial civil servants have tended to become civil masters. In all these systems, the managers have not only influence but power which does not always involve public accountability. This, indeed, is convergence.

While the first two convergence theses deal with the conditions of production, the third thesis deals with the conditions of consumption. It asserts that affluence tends to equalize and make similar the cultures of peoples who are subjected to different social systems. This thesis, which is derived from the superficial observation of "mass culture" and its diffusion, tends to ignore that "what people think, not what they consume or how they are forced to consume it," is an important determinant of culture. There are major cultural differences among the peoples of the Third World despite our poverty.

The convergence thesis tends to be restricted to a comparative evaluation of United States and U.S.S.R. political behaviour and responses. When the model generated by the thesis is extended to developing countries, the result points to a unidirectional process of cultural development that gives no comfort to any assertion of national, cultural autonomy. The theory of cultural dynamics is more complex than this.

Veblen[37] propounded the thesis that the social super-structure—politics, religion, morals and general habits of thought—is technologically determined; and that it derives its characteristics from the prevailing technology and techniques of production. It follows from this that the social superstructure changes as the technology changes. Recent work in industrial organization and management points to some elements of selective convergence. The argument is that the 'logic of industrialism' inevitably leads to a convergence in techniques, and through it to work habits, which cut through and undermine "tradition," irrespective of the main features of culture, history, and values with which the industrial society began.[38] Typical areas of convergence include:

(a) work specialization requiring scientific training and education;

(b) occupational professionalization;
(c) flexibility and mobility of labour;
(d) a reward or compensation system geared to rational economic contribution;
(e) proliferation of economic bargaining;
(f) all-pervasive ethic of the value of science and scientific innovation and
(g) diffusion of political power in society.

Japan is the only non-Western nation which has industrialized and competes in its own right in the world market. It provides a test case of the process of convergence. Japan ranks third in the World in G.N.P.; it is first in steel production and in ship-building; and second in automobiles and trucks. Employment in Japan's agricultural sector dropped from 40 percent of the labour force in 1955 to 22.5 percent in 1966 and currently it is around 17 percent of the labour force. This economic transformation is matched by its spatial transition: 50 percent of Japan's population was living in 1.25 percent of the country's area in 1966. Japan's balance of payments surpluses are a political embarrassment to Japan's leaders and an economic and political threat to many of its major international trading partner-countries. Industrially and economically Japan has arrived!

What is the evidence for or against convergence in Japan? The picture is mixed. Traditional institutions which governed labour relations in Japan have been undermined but are not dead. *Nemko* wages, *nemko* promotion and permanent employment have been the three pillars of the Japanese system of rewarding labour. But the tightening labour market and the introduction of new production technologies requiring highly trained, skilled labour challenge Japan's traditional system of rewarding labour. But more important, the basic value system of Japan remains substantially unchanged; and many of the foreign cultural institutions have been re-interpreted.

## Cultural Convergence and Dependency Theory: A Restatement

The pursuit of development demands cultural concession—concession to the traditions of the developing country as well as concession by it to the requirements of technical progress. The fact that developing countries must draw from the same basic ideas of science, management theory and technology in the solution of basically common problems of production and distribution, is a strong argument for convergence theory.

Cultural convergence is rooted in the relatively common effects of similar economic and political choices which the history and the character of the Third World countries impose upon their peoples. Its central thesis argues that, almost everywhere, common choices made under similar prevailing constraints, whether that of ideology, or technology, tend to generate similar structural and cultural patterns. The evidence from the Western African region suggests that while similar structural patterns are emerging in response to common constraints, their cultural content tends to be divergent.[39]

The irony of dependency theory, in cultural terms, is that it is not necessarily in defence of national cultural autonomy. It is an argument for socialism rather than capitalism, an argument that anticipates a new social formation based on a new value system. The new social system and the value system which supports it will tend to converge with the value system of the East and diverge away from the value system of the West and the original value system of the changing African society.

Convergent cultures may be *assimilative* or *integrative*. They are assimilative when dependent societies adopt the culture of the metropole; and integrative when they share the central cultural goals of the metropole but retain autonomy as to choice of cultural methods for achieving them. Assimilative convergence involves more cost than integrative convergence. From the point of view of exchange theory, the latter is a more rewarding relationship than the former. A more rewarding or good relationship is one in which the rewards exceed the costs. If we define reward as a transfer of resources from one culture to another, and cost as a resource taken away or denied, it will be clear that it is not the absolute size of the resource exchanged but the meaning of the exchange that determines if it is a reward or a cost. The *meaning* of an exchange depends on two factors: (a) the expectations, and (b) the manifest or perceived consequences of exchange. Dependency theory makes the point that the relationship between the Third World and the capitalist world is exploitative. This, in fact, is not a new observation. One of the findings of exchange theory is that the greater the heterogeneity within a given social system, the greater the probability that interactions will be costly. While West Africa's interactions with the Western world is demonstrably costly in political, economic, and cultural terms, there is no evidence from dependency theory that it will be less costly in any other system. In practically all the Western African countries, our focus for this workshop, the minority populations feel, and often can demonstrate, that their interaction with the dominant populations is costly to them. Dependency as an analytic tool, must remain a relative term.

The World is still far away from the convergence of the assimilative type. Everywhere, there is evidence of the integrative type of convergence. The demand for efficiency and the expanding network and penetrating power of bureaucracy are two important examples of the integrative type of convergence. They have not respected the boundaries of ideology, culture or policy in their growth and diffusion process.

Cultural convergence recognizes the fact of interdependence at all levels of the social system and tries to assess its social and cultural cost. Dependency theory ignores interdependence and the probable benefits flowing from it. By insisting on structural independence as the only path to Third World development, and ignoring the maldistribution of resource endowment among the Third World countries, dependency theory raises a false hope for development for many poor countries. The "single factor" magic for societal development is a prescription for disaster. Development is a complex process. Dependency theory cannot ignore the managerial irresponsibility demonstrated by many

Third World countries in the brief period of their political independence. Equally, too, it cannot underplay the necessary cultural adjustments we must make no matter what strategy of development is forced on the Third World.

## BIBLIOGRAPHY

AMIN, SAMIR. *Unequal Development.* Sussex, England, 1976.

BARAN, P. A. and SWEEZY, P. M. *Monopoly Capital.* England: Penguin, 1960.

BARNET, R. J. and MULLER, R. E. *Global Reach: The Power of Multinational Corporations.* New York, 1974.

BECKFORD, GEORGE L. *Persistent Poverty: Underdevelopment in Plantation Economies of the Third World.* London: Oxford University Press, 1972.

BENDIX, R. *Nation Building and Citizenship.* New York, 1964.

BOEKE, J. H. *Economics and Economic Policy of Dual Societies.* New York: Institute of Pacific Relations, 1953.

BRENNER, R. "The Origin of Capitalist Development: Critique of Neo-Smithian Marxism." *New Left Review* 104 (1977):25-92.

CHODAK, S. *Societal Development (Five Approaches).* New York: Oxford University Press, 1973.

DUMONT, R. *False Start in Africa.* London: Andre Deutsch, 1966.

FRANK, A. G. *Latin America: Underdevelopment or Revolution?* New York, 1969.

——. *Lumpenbourgeoisie: Lumpendevelopment: Dependence, Class and Politics in Latin America.* New York: Monthly Review Press, 1972.

GALTUNG, JOHAN. "A Structural Theory of Imperialism." *Journal of Peace Research,* 1971, pp. 81-118.

GEERTZ, C. *The Interpretation of Cultures.* London: Hutchinson, 1973.

HOPKINS, A. G. "Clio-Antics. A Horoscope for African Economic History." In *African Studies Since 1945: A Tribute to Basil Davidson.* Edited by C. Fyte. London: Longmans, 1976, pp. 31-44.

KARSH, B. and COLE, E. "Industrialization and the Convergence Hypothesis: Some Aspects of Contemporary Japan." *Journal of Social Issues* XXIV (1968): 45-64.

LEVINE, D. N. "The Flexibility of Traditional Cultures." *Journal of Social Issues* XXIV (1968): 129-141.

MAFEJE, A. "The Fallacy of Dual Economies Revisited." In *Dualism and Rural Development in East Africa.* Edited by P. Kongstad. Copenhagen: Insitute for Development Research, Denmark, 1973.

——. "The Fallacy of Dual Economies." *East Africa Journal,* 1972, pp. 7-9.

MAZRUI, A. A. *A World Federation of Cultures: (An African Perspective).* New York: The Free Press, 1976.

MEYER, G. G. "Theories of Convergence." In *Changes in Communist Systems.* Edited by C. Johnson. Stanford University Press, 1965.

OKONJO, C. "Economic Science, Imperialism and Nigerian Development: An Inaugural Lecture." Mimeographed. Nsukka, 1976.

PARSONS, T. *The Social System.* New York: The Free Press, 1951.

RODNEY, W. *How Europe Underdeveloped Africa.* London/Dar es Salaam, 1972.

ROSTOW, W. W. *The Stages of Economic Growth: A Non-Communist Manifesto.* Cambridge University Press, 1960.

SANTOS, THEOTONIO DOS. "The Structure of Dependence." *American Economic Review* LX (1970): 231-236.

TRIANDIS, H. C. "The Future of Pluralism." *Journal of Social Issues* 32 (1976):179-208.

UCHENDU, V. C. "Polity Primacy and African Economic Development." *Proceedings, Universities of East Africa Social Science Conference,* 1969.

——. "The Challenge of Cultural Transitions in Sub-Saharan Africa." *The Annals—American Academy of Political and Social Sciences* 432 (1977):70-79.

VAN PEURSEN, G. A. *The Strategy of Culture.* Amsterdam, 1974.
VEBLEN, T. *The Impact of Workmanship and the State of Industrial Arts.* New York: Macmillan, 1914.
WALLERSTEIN, I. "Dependence in an Interdependent World: The Limited Possibilities of Transformation within the Capitalist World Economy." *African Studies Review* XVII (1974):1-27.
——. *The Origins of the Modern World Systems.* New York, 1974.
WILES, P. "Will Capitalism and Communism Spontaneously Converge?" *ENCOUNTER* XXI (1963):84-90.

## NOTES

1   Rostow, *The Stages of Economic Growth: A Non-Communist Manifesto,* Cambridge University Press, 1960.
2   Rostow, *The Stages of Economic Growth,* 1960, p. 4.
3   Rostow, Ibid., 1960, p. 8.
4   Dumont, *False Start in Africa,* London, 1966.
5   Boeke, *Economics and Economic Policy of Dual Societies,* New York, 1953, p. 5-6.
6   Mafejeh, "The Fallacy of Dual Economies Revisited," *Dualism and Rural Development in East Africa,* Institute for Development Research, Denmark, 1973; "The Fallacy of Dual Economies," *East Africa Journal,* 1972, pp. 7-9.
7   Rodney, *How Europe Underdeveloped Africa,* London/Dar-es-Salaam, 1972.
8   Beckford, *Persistent Poverty,* London, Oxford University Press, 1972.
9   Amin, *Unequal Development,* Sussex, England, 1976, p. 10.
10  Santos, "The Structure of Dependence," *American Economic Review,* 1970, p. 231.
11  Santos, Ibid., 1970, p. 231-234.
12  Okonjo, "Economic Science, Imperialism and Nigerian Development," [An Inaugural Lecture], (Mimeo), Nsukka, Nigeria, 1976.
13  Galtung, "A Structural Theory of Imperialism," *Journal of Peace Research,* 1971, pp. 81-118.
14  Frank, *Latin America: Underdevelopment or Revolution,* New York, 1969, ix, 4, 9.
15  Frank, Ibid., 1969, p. 6.
16  Rodney, op. cit., 1972, p. 22.
17  Rodney, Ibid., 1972, p. 17.
18  Amin, op. cit., 1976, p. 22.
19  Wallerstein, "Dependence in an Interdependent World: The Limited Possibilities of Transformation within the Capitalist World Economy," *African Studies Review,* 1974, p. 2.
20  Frank, op. cit., 1969, p. 5.
21  Frank, Ibid., 1969, p. 4.
22  Frank, Ibid., 1969, p. 9.
23  Baran and Sweezy, *Monopoly Capital,* Penguin Books, England, 1966, p. 12.
24  Rodney, op. cit., 1972, p. 7.
25  Barnet and Muller, *Global Reach: The Power of Multi-national Corporations,* New York, 1974, p. 25; Baran and Sweezy, op. cit., 1966, p. 58.
26  Hopkins, "Clio-Antics: A Horoscope for African Economic History," in C. Fyte (ed.) *African Studies Since 1945: A Tribute to Basil Davidson,* London, Longmans, 1976.
27  Uchendu, "Polity Primacy and African Economic Development," *Proceedings: Universities of East Africa Social Science Conference,* Nairobi, 1969.
28  Triandis, "The Future of Pluralism," *Journal of Social Issues,* Vol. 32, No. 4, 1976.
29  Geertz, *The Interpretation of Cultures,* London, 1973.
30  Uchendu, "The Challenge of Cultural Transitions in Sub-Saharan Africa," *The Annals of American Academy of Political and Social Science,* Vol. 432, 1977, pp. 71-2; See also Van Peursen, *The Strategy of Culture,* Amsterdam, North Holland Publishing Company, 1974, pp. 11-140.
31  Parsons, *The Social System,* New York, The Free Press of Glencoe 1951.
32  Wiles, "Will Capitalism and Communism Spontaneously Converge?" *Encounter,* Vol. xxi, 1963, pp. 84-90.

33  Wiles, Ibid., 1963, p. 84.
34  Wiles, Ibid., 1963, p. 85.
35  Wiles, Ibid., 1963, p. 85.
36  Wiles, Ibid.
37  Veblen, *The Instinct of Workmanship and the State of Industrial Arts,* New York, Macmillan, 1914.
38  Karsh and Cole, "Industrialization and the Convergence Hypothesis: Some Aspects of Contemporary Japan," *Journal of Social Issues,* Vol. xxiv, No. 4, 1968, pp. 45-64.
39  Uchendu, op. cit., 1977, pp. 77-78.

# PART III

# INSTITUTIONAL RESPONSES TO METROPOLITAN STRUCTURES OF DOMINATION

# The 'Received' Nigerian Law and the Challenge of Legal Independence

S. N. NWABARA

*Institute of African Studies, University of Nigeria, Nsukka, Nigeria*

THERE IS NOT JUST ONE 'RECEIVED' LAW[1] in Nigeria. On the contrary, Nigeria has two 'imported' laws—the Common Law and the Islamic Law of the Maliki School. How these two imported laws impact upon our legal system is the main theme of this paper.

## Introduction of the English Law

The period 1472 to 1833 marked a concerted interaction between the coastal chiefs of Nigeria and the Europeans—notably the Portuguese and the British. But after 1833—the year of the abolition of the slave trade—the interaction assumed a different phase. Indeed, the Portuguese were elbowed out by the British. Within that period both the Portuguese and the English, in their respective periods, were subject to the various systems of Nigerian laws which regulated their business, and except for any 'treaty' laws in operation, foreign laws had no auspicious effect on the peoples of the coastal areas.

From 1833 onwards it was a different case. The so-called peaceful trade was established principally in palm produce, and interaction with the people of Nigeria was no longer a matter of chance. Having out-smarted King Docemo of Lagos Island, the British induced him to cede Lagos to the British Crown on 6 August 1861 and consequently, Britain established a strong foothold on the coast of Nigeria. Lagos was declared 'Colony and Settlement' in 1862 with H. S. Freeman as Governor, and also Consul for Fernando Po.[2] Thus a kind of court was inaugurated empowering the Governor to settle disputes between the local inhabitants.[3] Freeman's first judicial enactment was the establishment of a police magistrate court for Lagos at Olowegbowo to be guided by the law that was in force in England as at 1 January 1863. The court was removed to Tinubu Square on 25 June 1869.[4] A month later, another ordinance followed. This was an "ordinance to provide for the better administration of Justice within the Settlement of Lagos." Its first judge was a Chief Magistrate and by February 1862, the court was presided over by a Chief Justice.[5]

In the opinion of this author, the beginning of the introduction of English

Law in Nigeria dated from this period. The British did not seem to favour the trend of events in West Africa, because of what appeared as over-centralization of the West African Settlements.[6] These Settlements had a legislative council with headquarters in Freetown under a governor-in-chief. A select Committee of the House of Commons advised early withdrawal from the West African Coast "leaving the inhabitants to govern themselves while the British devoted themselves to the promotion of legitimate trade."[7] This policy not withstanding, there was a reorganization of the Settlements. By Ordinance No. 7 of December 1866, a Supreme Court was established in Sierra Leone which handled appeals from the court of civil and criminal Justice of other Settlements. Appeals from Sierra Leone went to the Judicial Committee of the Privy Council in England, thus making Sierra Leone the centre of West African Court of Appeal. However, in 1874, Lagos and Gold Coast were excised from Sierra Leone, but Lagos remained administratively a part of the Eastern Province of Gold Coast[8] until 1886.

While Lagos was still being administered from Gold Coast, two Ordinances were enacted—the Supreme Court Ordinance No. 4 of 1876 and the Criminal Procedure Ordinance No. 5 of 1876 which, according to Elias, laid the foundations of the modern legal system in Nigeria. The Supreme Court Ordinance is important to us because, even though it upheld the supremacy of the Law and practice for the time being in force in England, it also provided for the "observance and application of native law and custom not repugnant to the principle of justice, equity and good conscience." It reads in part:[9]

> Nothing in this Ordinance shall deprive the Supreme Court of the right to observe and enforce the observance, or shall deprive any person of the benefit, of any law or custom existing in the said Colony and territories subject to its jurisdiction, such law or custom not being repugnant to natural justice, equity and good conscience, nor incompatible either directly or by necessary implication with any enactment of the Colonial Legislature existing at the Commencement of this Ordinance, or which may afterwards come into operation.

The formation of the National African Company Limited in 1882 to take over the business of the United African Company Limited in Central and East Africa and in the Niger Regions was a landmark not only in commercial enterprise and contact with the Africans but also in the establishment of a commercial empire which eventually placed Britain on the economic map of West Africa. Having purchased the business of Campagnie Francaise de l'Afrique Equatoriale, the way was clear for Consul Edward Hyde Hewett to conclude treaties with the chiefs of the Niger District which placed their territories under British protection.

Our interest is not in the political and diplomatic 'juggling' between the French, the German and the British in delineating spheres of commercial influence but in the treaties which the British concluded with the various peoples of Nigeria in the late nineteenth century. The National African Company (Limited) concluded not less than thirty-nine treaties with the Niger district chiefs in 1884. While the chiefs were said to have ceded the whole of their respective territories to the company by various Acts of Cession specified in the schedule, an important clause was further elaborated to read "in consideration of this [ceding the whole of their territory to the company], the National African Company (Limited) will not interfere with any of the native laws, and also not encroach on any private property unless the value is agreed upon by the owner and the said company."[10] By 1877 the area from Lagos to Benue was under British protection with all the paraphernalia of government. Chief Justice Marshall was naturally the lord of all the courts of justice established within the area. The Royal Charter of 1886, granted to Taubman Goldie's Niger Company, was specific on its legal relations with the people. It in part reads:

> In the administration of justice by the Company to the peoples of its territories, or to any of the inhabitants thereof, careful regard shall always be had to the customs and laws of the class, or tribe, or nation to which the parties respectively belong, especially with respect to the holding, possession, transfer, and disposition of lands and goods, and testate or intestate succession thereto, and marriage, divorce, and legitimacy, and other rights or property and personal rights.[11]

T. O. Elias sees the above as the germ that underlay all subsequent policy towards customary law and which excludes certain aspects of indigenous customary laws from the jurisdiction of British-established courts. But it is also the central argument for the doctrine of 'Repugnancy' which submerged customary laws under English laws and sentenced African law and custom to perpetual servitude.

When in 1900 the British government took over the administration of Nigeria from the Royal Niger Company, two parallel tribunals were established in the northern and southern Nigeria, respectively, to serve the judicial needs of the peoples in those areas. In the North, Sir Fredrick Lugard, who had utilized the Emirate machinery to advantage, viewed with disgust the Southern Tribunal and therefore dreamed of a day when he would be on the saddle of Nigerian power. His dream was realized in 1914—the year when the two protectorates were amalgamated and he became Governor-General.

Lugard recognized the existence and role of native law and custom as a means of maintaining law and order, but went further to justify his conviction by according recognition to chiefs administering customary laws in Nigerian courts. About this he said:

> The position and authority of 'recognized chiefs' has been safeguarded by several enactments. The Native Courts Ordinance (No. 8 of 1914) enforced Native law and custom, confers on Native Tribunals powers of arrest, and imposes upon them the duty of maintaining order (Sections 18 and 19). They may make Rules with the concurrence of the Head Chief, and the approval of the Governor, with the object of adding to Native customary law, so as to enable the Courts to take cognizance of offences against Native Law, and otherwise to maintain good order, and to promote the welfare of the Natives.[12]

A year after, he launched his uniform system of Native Tribunal with an air of accomplishment and pride:

> Under the Native Courts Ordinance, 1914, amended by No. 15 of 1915, a uniform system of Native Tribunals has been established throughout Nigeria but, as in all other matters of

administration, the diversity of conditions is so great in this vast country that the general principles laid down in the Ordinance must be adapted to the circumstances of the different Provinces.[13]

Lugard's recognition of the authority of chiefs and the place he gave native tradition in his scheme of administration should not be construed to mean equality of the customary law with the English law. Such conception would, in theory and practice, be repugnant, as indeed it was, to all colonial administrations. In the typical colonial mentality that  prevailed, there was no conflict between the "policy of preserving indigenous institutions and that of superimposing an alien culture."[14] On the contrary, the colonial legal system made it clear that certain aspects of Nigerian cultural traditions and institutions were 'repugnant', and this was the beginning of the erosion of Nigerian culture by alien influence. Aware of this cultural erosion, Margery Perham's consolation to Nigerians is worth citing, "This [superimposing of alien culture] need not be regretted when we remember that the preservation of native law and custom is not an end in itself, but a transitional stage by means of which Africans may in their own right become members of the civilized world, not as individuals, but as communities."[15]

## The Principle of Repugnancy

T. O. Elias distinguishes two types of recognition of customary law in relation to British colonial policy. First, when the customary law was well established and ascertainable, recognition was undisputed and second, where the community was 'politically' unorganized and 'uncivilized', recognition was vague and tardy.[16] He further stated that a colonial judge was enjoined to uphold a rule of customary law that was not "repugnant to natural justice, equity and good conscience." Elias did not lose sight of the fact that by the provision of 'repugnancy clause' the colonial masters became arbiters of what was true, honourable, just, lovely and gracious in native law and custom. He asks, "...by what criteria is he (the colonial judge) to determine the issue?"[17] Elias spoke the mind of many Africans when he said, "The broad statement of legal policy does not exclude the possibility of occasional but wrongful application of English legal ideas in the determination of alien issues."[18] Nor was he the only eminent Nigerian jurist to frown upon the repugnancy clause. Ademola, C.J.F., in Kano N.A. versus R. A. Obiora, declared that the procedure in native courts was not contrary to natural justice merely because it was foreign to English law.[19] Chief Magistrate Onyechi called attention to the importance of that declaration. He said, "This was a Nigerian Judge pointing a way out of the bondage allotted to customary law by the colonialists."[20] Continuing, Onyechi remarked almost bitterly that judicial law had "interpreted the repugnancy rule as it affected the applicability of a rule of customary law in such a way as to show that it was the English standard that was required".[21]

It is no exaggeration that there is hardly any facet of customary rule that has not been affected to the point of denigration by the 'received' laws. Ostensibly one of the customary rules that readily comes to mind is marriage. Under the Islamic law, for example, the Sharia controls the dispensation of justice over Muslim personal law, that is, any question regarding marriage or family relationship or guardianship of an infant.[22] The dominance of judicial law over customary marriage rears up its head like a monster in Ordinance Marriage versus Customary Marriage. When, for example, two spouses marry under the two systems, it is the former that judicially holds sway in a country where polygyny is legally recognized. That both the Christian church and the government of Nigeria have recognized Ordinance marriage above Customary marriage is evidence of Nigerian legal dependency. More painful about the dominance of alien form of marriage is that Customary marriage does not entitle the woman to the property of a deceased husband. Yet the dual system of marriage has come to stay in Nigeria particularly in the predominantly Christian south where some Christians abhor Ordinance marriage. Unfortunately there is no relief in sight in regard to the abolition of the legal dualism in which the alien form takes precedence.

The most recent example of legal dependency as it affects customary law is in respect of land tenure—the *Land Use Decree*. The generally accepted principle of land tenure in Southern Nigeria is that "...the farms are held by adult men individually and most men of middle age have well established rights to perhaps half a dozen sets of plots."[23] When in 1911 government wanted to formulate legislation in regard to land tax, the recommendation by a senior District Officer that government should assume the control of all lands in the central and eastern provinces,[24] was turned down because it conflicted with native land tenure as it applied to those provinces, even though in the north the Emirs acted as "trustees of the land on behalf of the people to whom the land belonged."[25] The customary courts of the south were clothed with "unlimited jurisdiction in causes and matters concerning the ownership, possession or occupation of land."[26] Similarly, the Area Courts Edict of Northern States of Nigeria states that "in land causes and matters the native law and custom to be applied by an area court shall be the native law and custom in force in relation to land in the place where the land is situated."[27] This provision is very important in view of the fact that land in Northern Nigeria is vested in the Emir who holds it in trust for the people.

The age-long tradition of land-holding in Nigeria which had, particularly in the south, formed a significant economic basis was eroded and almost destroyed by the recent *Land Use Decree* promulgated by the government.[28] Paragraph one states:

> All land comprised in the territory of each state in the Federation are hereby vested in the Military Governor of that state and such land shall be held in trust and administered for the use and common benefit of all Nigerians.[29]

The Decree claims that it is "...in the public interest that the rights of all Nigerians to the land of Nigeria be asserted and preserved by law."[30] This language presupposes the non-existence of land tenure law in Nigeria prior to the Decree and suggests that under the Decree any person could own or enter any piece of land without regard to customary land tenure of that part of Nigeria in which the land is situated.

What the Decree has therefore done is not only to alienate proprietory rights of land ownership from the people by transferring such rights to the states, but also—and this is crucial—to deny land owners a vital economic source of revenue. For example, there are many people today in Nigeria whose parents or guardians used their land as a collateral for loans which enabled them to put their children through primary, post-primary or university education. Following the completion of their education, the children saved up money to redeem the land. To my mind the Decree has achieved two retrogressive objectives: perpetuation of legal dependency by eroding customary law and economic dependency by attacking a vital source of the people's income.

Further, the Decree seems a recrudescense of the land expropriation in northern Nigeria by the British in the beginning of this century. The British aped the Fulani, who, on the application of the Islamic law of the Maliki school, treated on conquest all cultivated lands as 'Wakf', but such lands reverted to the owners if they became Muslims, while all other lands belonged to the Emir. As we shall see later, the Emirs granted fiefs to some followers in return for tax based on one-tenth of the produce.

Upon assumption of authority over the northern territory of Nigeria, the British contemplated collecting economic rent on land since, like the Emir, the State was now the owner of the land. The Northern Nigeria Land Committee whose report appeared in 1910 affirmed that the "...ultimate ownership of the land was vested in the chiefs and had been acquired by the British by conquest, but rights so acquired should be exercised for the use of common benefit of Africans and in accordance with native law."[31] The Committee, however, advised against 'economic' rent on the grounds that it was contrary to custom for the State to take rent for land. Subsequent proclamations evoked criticisms which are still apt today, namely: first, 'ultimate ownership' of land was looked upon as expropriation and second, the notion that "no title to the occupation of land would be valid without the Governor's assent would have the effect of rendering customary occupation invalid."[32]

## Islamic Law

We have seen how, under the Islamic law of the Maliki School, land was expropriated from non-Muslims, and by English legal interpretation, an identical measure was contemplated by the British following the conquest of the Fulani of Northern Nigeria. But the Islamic Law has been so assimilated in some parts of Nigeria that sight has been lost of it as another 'received' law. Though in land tenure the Area Courts Edict provides for Customary usage as the basis for determination, invariably this applies where non-Muslims are involved in a dispute over land causes and matters.

Islam did not thrive in a vacuum in Northern Nigeria. Before the Jihad was unleashed on the Hausa kingdoms in the early nineteenth century, the people had a well-developed economy with a social system based either on hereditary or non-hereditary clientage.[33] The Fulani conquerors married themselves to the two systems, modifying them along the way. "The Fulbe," according to J. S. Trimingham, "adopted the existing state structure with its wealth of dignitaries together with their Hausa titles. Successful flag-invested clerics were recognized by Uthman as fief holders."[34]

Fief holders' main task was the collection of taxes from their fiefs, and, therefore, they had the power to appoint and depose minor district or village chiefs. The fact that the clerics were fief-holders or tax collectors should not be interpreted to mean that Uthman employed the Jihad as a camouflage for mercenary venture. The impression of mercenary motive underlying the Jihad was created by what appeared like a repetition of the scramble for loot that characterized Islam in decades following the death of the prophet Mohammed. Trimingham observes that the "...fruits of power sapped the vital energies that brought such success and the *Jihad* degenerated into undisguised slave-raiding which together with perpetual wars ruined and depopulated vast areas."[35]

The point to be borne in mind is that the Islamic entry into Habe states was not a clarion call for clientage or vassalage. This social system was in existence prior to Islam but it equally suited mercenary-minded Muslims who unfortunately perpetuated the system.

The fundamental issue in Islam is the pre-eminence of Islamic law and the grip which religion has on the law itself. In other words, Islam and Islamic law are props that support each other. Lewis has put it more succinctly: "As far as the character of West African Islam is concerned, it is important to note the strong emphasis placed on the law as the basis of Islam, its connection with the rise of centralized states, and its eventual fulfillment in Theocratic rule."[36] Thus the Muslims claim legitimacy on the interpretation of the Sharia in their economic, social and political reforms if, and even where, such changes were opposed to their interests. "Islamic law may be applied," wrote Lewis, "...to circumvent onerous traditional obligations towards kinsfolk, converts to Islam taking advantage of their new legal position to deny specific kinsmen a share in newly acquired wealth."[37] The Sharia is therefore 'all things to all men', and certain norms could be upheld or cast aside with justification on a strict interpretation of the Sharia. On the whole, Islamic law—the Sharia—in its application could influence and sustain independence or perpetuate dependency. It is a dichotomy, and according to Lewis:

> This dichotomy which enables Muslims, if not Islam as such, to accommodate so much and so variously, not only of traditional but also of new influences, is not always adequately expressed in such terms as 'dualism' and 'parallelism' etc. For the strength of Muslim devotion, at least in many areas, is still such that in the last analysis these two distinct sources of legitimacy are seen as merging in a single Muslim way of life where all standards of thought and conduct are assumed to derive their final sanctity.[38]

## The Challenge

The challenge posed by the 'Received Law' to Nigerian legal independence is not different from the challenge of socio-economic independence, or educational independence. What has been described as 'colonial mentality' is so endemic in Nigeria that many Nigerians are more 'English' than the English. Everything 'English' is regarded as superior to its indigenous counterpart. The entire whiteman's life style is adored: so it is not a surprise that in the area of legal process Nigeria should prefer English and Islamic Law—two received laws—to Customary law—the only law that should claim legitimacy.

Again Onyechi cries aloud for legal independence:

> The citizens must be truly presumed to know the law so that the justice of the law courts would bring to them substantial justice, properly so called. The attraction seems to weigh heavily in favour of indigenizing Nigeria law. Alien law would assume its position as foreign Law. The aboriginal law would cease to be foreign to its birth-place. The country and the citizen would be endowed with Justice and Peace. Law and Order would prevail. There would be the birth of a Nation.[39]

The problem goes farther than meets the eye. Reading through the National Development Plans, particularly the second and third Plans (1970-74, 1975-80), one is shocked by the apparent lack of a plan for a national law. Paragraph eight of the Third National Plan states that "serious effort has been made to emphasize those sectors which directly affect the *welfare* [Italics ours] of the ordinary citizen,"[40] and they include housing, water supplies, health, education, rural electrification and community development. It further identifies at paragraph twelve four broad sectors one of which is economic. This is fair enough because emphasis is laid on the welfare of the ordinary citizen, but it is humbly submitted that any scheme of welfare that does not provide for cultural dimensions will result in quantitative rather than qualitative growth. But we must demand both. In other words, any planning, be it economic or otherwise, must be rooted in the people's culture in all its ramifications—the indigenous law not excepted. Only then can the challenge of the 'received' law *vis a vis* Nigerian independence be countered.

## BIBLIOGRAPHY

Azikiwe, N. *Land Tenure in Northern Nigeria.* Lagos: African Book Company, 1942.
Balonwu, M. O. "The Growth and Development of Indigenous Nigerian Laws as Part of Our Heritage From British Colonial Rule." In *African Indigenous Laws.* Edited by T. O. Elias, et al. Enugu: Government Printer, 1975.
Daniels, W. G. Ekow. *The Common Law in West Africa.* London: Butterworth, 1964.
Elias, T. O. *British Colonial Law. A Comparative Study of the Interactions between English and Local Laws in British Dependencies.* London: Stevens & Sons, 1962.
Elias, T. O., et al., eds. *African Indigenous Laws.* Enugu: Government Printer, 1975.
Hailey, Lord. *An African Survey.* London: Oxford University Press, 1956 edition.
Hertslet, E. *The Map of Africa by Treaty.* London: Frank Cass, 1967 edition.

Kirk-Greene, A. H. M. *Lord Lugard: Political Memoranda 1913-1918.* London: Frank Cass, 1970.
Lewis, I. M. *Islam in Tropical Africa.* London: Oxford University Press, 1969.
Meek, C. K. *Land Law and Custom in the Colonies.* London: Oxford University Press, 1946.
Nigeria, Eastern. *The Laws of Eastern Nigeria.* Enugu, 1956.
Nigeria, Federal. *Land Use Decree 1978, No. 6.* Lagos, 1978.
——. *Development Plan 1975-80.* Lagos: Ministry of Economic Development, 1976.
Nigeria, Northern. *The Laws of Northern Nigeria.* Kaduna: Sharia Appeal Court, 1965.
——. *The Area Courts Edict of Northern States of Nigeria.* Kaduna: Government Printer, 1975.
Nwabara, S. N. *Iboland: A Century of Contact with Britain 1860-1960.* London: Holder & Stoughton, 1977.
Onyechi, J. N. M. "A Problem of Assimilation or Dominance?" *African Indigenous Laws.* Edited by T. O. Elias, et al. Enugu, 1975.
Perham, Margery. *Colonial Sequence 1930-1949.* London: Methuen, 1967.
Shaban, M. A. *Islamic History: A New Interpretation A.D. 600-750.* Cambridge: University Press, 1976.
Smith, M. G. *Government in Zazzau.* London: Oxford University Press, 1960.
Trimingham, J. S. *A History of Islam in West Africa.* London: Oxford University Press, 1974.

## NOTES

1 'Received' Law in this paper is the 'English' Law which consists of three elements—common law, equity and statutes. See W. C. Ekow Daniels, *Common Law in West Africa,* London, Butterworth, 1964, p. 110.
2 Elias, *Nigeria: The Development of its Laws and Constitution,* London, Stevens and Sons, 1967, p. 7. The British had by 1886 declared a protectorate over Yorubaland except Abeokuta and in 1893 signed a treaty by which Egbaland was recognized as an independent state with its own administration.
3 Elias, Ibid., 1967, p. 18.
4 Elias, Ibid., 1967, The Ordinance empowering the application of English Law at Olowogbowo Court was to take effect from 4 March 1863.
5 Elias, Ibid., 1967.
6 Elias, Ibid., 1967, The Settlements comprised Gold Coast (Ghana), Gambia, Sierra Leone and Lagos.
7 Elias, Ibid., 1967.
8 Daniels, *The Common Law in West Africa,* London, Butterworth, 1964, p. 37.
9 Hertslet, *The Map of Africa by Treaty,* London, Frank Cass, 1967, p. 116.
10 Hertslet, Ibid., 1967, p. 137.
11 Cited in Elias, *Nigeria,* 1967, p. 20. See also Justice M. O. Balonwu "The Growth and Development of Indigenous Nigerian Laws as Part of our Heritage from the British Colonial Rule," in Elias, *et. al.* (ed.), *African Indigenous Laws,* Enugu, Government Printer, 1975, p. 32.
12 Kirk-Greene, *Lord Lugard: Political Memoranda,* London, Frank Cass, 1970, p. 299.
13 Kirk-Greene, Ibid., 1970, p. 205. See the 'Memo No. VIII-Native Courts'.
14 Perham, *Colonial Sequence 1930-1949,* London, Methuen, 1967, p. 64.
15 Perham, Ibid., 1967, p. 65.
16 Elias, *British Colonial Law; A Comparative Study of the Interactions between English and Local Laws in British Dependencies,* London, Stevens & Sons, 1962, p. 101.
17 Elias, Ibid., 1962, p. 104.
18 Elias, Ibid., 1962.
19 Cited in Onyechi, "A Problem of Assimilation or Dominance," *African Indigenous Laws,* Enugu Government Printer, 1975, p. 276.
20 Onyechi, Ibid., 1975, p. 277.
21 Onyechi, Ibid., 1975, p. 276.

22   *The Laws of Northern Nigeria,* cap. 22, "Sharia Court of Appeal," Kaduna, Government
     Printer, 1965, p. 1936.
23   Meek, *Land Law and Customs in the Colonies,* London, O.U.P., 1946, pp. 145-168.
24   Nwabara, *Iboland: A Century of Contact with Britain, 1860-1960,* London, Hodder and Stough-
     ton, 1977, p. 38.
25   Nnamdi Azikiwe, *Land Tenure in Northern Nigeria,* Lagos, African Book Company, 1942,
     p. 8.
26   *Eastern Region of Nigeria, Laws of, 21 of 1956, cap. 32, First Schedule II.*
27   *The Area Courts Edict of Northern States of Nigeria,* Kaduna, Government Printer, 1975, All,
     21(2).
28   *Nigeria, Land Use Decree 1978,* Decree No. 6, Lagos, Nigeria.
29   *Land Use Decree,* 1978, para. I.
30   Ibid.
31   Lord Hailey, *An African Survey,* London, O.U.P., 1956, pp. 733-4.
32   Hailey, Ibid., 1956, p. 734.
33   Smith, *Government in Zazzau,* Oxford, University Press, 1960, pp. 6-8; Shaban, *Islamic His-
     tory: A New Interpretation A.D. 600-750,* Cambridge, University Press, 1976, p. 11.
34   Trimingham, *A History of Islam in West Africa,* Oxford, University Press, 1974, p. 203.
35   Trimingham, Ibid., 1974, p. 205.
36   Lewis, *Islam in Tropical Africa,* Oxford, University Press, 1969, p. 18.
37   Lewis, Ibid., 1969, p. 49.
38   Lewis, Ibid., 1969, p. 75.
39   Onyechi, "A Problem of Assimilation or Dominance," *African Indigenous Laws,* Enugu,
     Government Printer, 1975, p. 259.
40   Nigeria, Federal, *Development Plan 1975-80,* (Lagos: Ministry of Economic Development,
     1976).

# ECOWAS:
# Is it a Countervailing Power for Economic Independence?

J. C. AGHAJI

*Institute of African Studies, University of Nigeria, Nsukka, Nigeria*

SINCE THE END OF THE SECOND WORLD WAR there has been a growing awareness among the nations of the world that regional economic integration is necessary for the promotion of economic development and intra-regional trade. The signing of the treaty of Rome in 1957, which established the European Economic Community, set an example of regional economic grouping which has not been ignored by the developing countries.

In the African context, the emergence of independent African States has brought into focus the economic limitations of national boundaries inherited at independence, boundaries which disrupt the continuities of trade, flows of factors of production and also common economic policies. Although the West African countries fully appreciate the trade-restraining effect of their national boundaries, yet they have been very slow indeed to respond to the challenges which these boundaries posed. This is a case where political sensitivity has overridden clearly perceived economic advantages.

The United Nations General Assembly in many of its resolutions, has urged all developing countries to continue their efforts at fostering regional and sub-regional integration in order to expand trade among themselves. Also, the United Nations Conference on Trade and Development (UNCTAD) since its inception has emphasized the need for developing countries to make real efforts to avail themselves of the opportunities presented for trade expansion and economic co-operation among themselves, both to foster their economic growth and also strengthen their overall position in relation to the developed countries. The United Nations Economic Commission for Africa (ECA) has not ignored the compelling economic necessity for cooperation within its region. It believes that the harmonization of industrial development within each sub-region of Africa or within a group of countries is the answer to Africa's development problems. The considerable amount of research on the economics of integration which the ECA has done in the regions of Africa strengthens its case.

## A Brief History

It is significant that the need for economic co-operation in Africa was felt long before the movement for political independence became a reality for most African countries.[1] The Pan-African Congress of 1945, held in Manchester, after noting the systematic exploitation of the economic resources of West Africa by the imperial powers, recommended *inter alia*, the establishment of a West African Economic Union. In apparent support of this view, the first conference of the political parties in Africa held in Accra in December 1958, also called for the removal of customs and other restrictions on trade between African States and the conclusion of multinational payments agreements, with a view to enhancing economic exchanges and consequent establishment of an African Common Market. The Organization of African Unity, in May 1973, at its tenth summit conference in Addis Ababa, adopted an African Declaration on Co-operation, Development and Economic Independence which, *inter alia*, urged African countries to step up inter-African co-operation particularly in the monetary and communications fields.

The pre-independence co-operative movements did not result in any important action. However, after the achievement of political independence West African countries intensified their efforts. Good examples are the West African Economic Community (CEAO) and the various bilateral trade agreements that exist today between the French-speaking West African States. But of great importance is the West African Clearing House which was launched on 1 July 1976, by the West African Sub-Regional Committee of the Association of African Central Banks, the first such Clearing House to be established in Africa. It takes care of the problems posed by the existence of different currency zones in West Africa by providing a facility through which members of the Clearing House could economize on the use of foreign exchange reserves and transfer costs. It would seem that both the Clearing House and ECOWAS stand out clearly as two very important post-independence co-operative schemes in that they embrace most of the countries in West Africa, thus transcending linguistic and cultural barriers.[2]

Despite this effort, the West African intra-regional trade is, to a large extent, still divided into two main zones, the French Franc Zone and the Sterling Area; and the intra-regional trade is still very small. It would appear that many of the factors which hindered intra-regional and inter-zonal trade before independence are still as strong as they were. Some of these are lack of adequate infrastructure by way of road, rail, telecommunications and other links for the movement of goods and persons, vested interests in the preservation of the *status quo*, the persistence of semi-colonial ties, the stronger economic pull towards past colonial masters in Europe than to other African countries in the region, the competitive structure of industries and natural resources, shortage of basic statistical data for reliable assessment of probable repercussions of the integration process, lack of political will to surrender some elements of the national sovereignty to a supra-national authority with powers to take economic and social decisions on behalf of the group. But the only significant development so far, it would seem, is the fact that West African countries are now getting much closer to the idea of establishing a customs union; and after some years of protracted negotiations, the Economic Community of West African States (ECOWAS) was established when its treaty was signed in Lagos on 28 May 1975. The question one may ask here is whether ECOWAS can provide a countervailing power or whether it is a neo-colonial instrument that will perpetuate dependence. Put differently: what are the probable effects of ECOWAS on West African economic development and intra-regional trade? In other words, to what extent can the community stimulate intra-regional trade and co-operation by altering its present pattern which is externally dependent? Will this course of action lead to the economic independence of the member states of the community?

The main objective of this paper is, therefore, to examine the probable effect of ECOWAS on West African trade, economic independence, and political integration. The paper is divided into three sections. Section I deals with the pre-ECOWAS pattern of economic development, Section II, the ECOWAS Treaty provisions and Section III, the effects of ECOWAS on the economic independence and political integration of the countries making up the community.

## Pre-ECOWAS Pattern of Economic Development

We have pointed out the chequered history of the integration process in West Africa up till the time of the inauguration of the ECOWAS in 1975, and the conceptual and practical difficulties encountered in the movements towards regional integration. There were two very important features of the West African trade. First, most of the foreign trades of individual countries in the sub-region were carried on with non-African countries, the intra-regional trade among West African States being insignificant. Second, the small amount of trade that takes place in the sub-region is largely on zonal basis, with little inter-zonal trade going on between the Anglophone countries of the Sterling area and the Francophone countries of the Franc area. In 1972, Nigeria and Togo, which belong to different currency zones, initiated an agreement for promoting through their joint endeavours, co-operation between themselves and also among West African countries. This is the beginning of ECOWAS and its Treaty is a tribute to the wisdom and positive response of West Africans to the political and economic needs of their region.

The sixteen member states of the ECOWAS, within the West African sub-region as defined by the United Nations Economic Commission for Africa (ECA), together occupy a geographical area of well over six million square kilometres and share among themselves a total population of about 124 million. However, they vary considerably in size, in geography and in population. The Gambia, which is the smallest of them, has an area of only 11, 295 square kilometres and a population of less than half a million. The correspon-

*Table I*

*Labour Force Utilization in Ecowas States*

| Member States | Population (in million) | Percentage in agri-culture | Percentage in industry and service | Main Export |
|---|---|---|---|---|
| Dahomey | 2.4 | 52.0 | 48.0 | Goundnut, palm kernel |
| Gambia | 0.4 | 78.0 | 22.0 | Groundnut |
| Ghana | 9.1 | 58.0 | 42.0 | Cocoa, bauxite |
| Guinea | 5.1 | 85.0 | 17.0 | Bauxite, iron ore |
| Guinea Bissau | 0.5 | 89.0 | 19.0 | Groundnut |
| Ivory Coast | 5.4 | 81.0 | 19.0 | Palm produce, cocoa, cotton |
| Liberia | 1.6 | 74.0 | 26.0 | Iron ore |
| Mali | 5.3 | 91.0 | 9.0 | Groundnut, cotton |
| Mauritania | 1.2 | 85.0 | 15.0 | Iron ore |
| Niger | 4.3 | 91.0 | 9.0 | Groundnut |
| Nigeria | 79.5 | 67.0 | 23.0 | Petroleum, cocoa groundnut |
| Senegal | 4.0 | 76.0 | 24.0 | Groundnut |
| Togo | 2.0 | 75.0 | 20.0 | Cotton |
| Sierra Leone | 2.7 | 74.0 | 26.0 | Diamond, groundnut |
| Upper Volta | 5.6 | 89.0 | 11.0 | Livestock |
| Cape Verde | n.a. | n.a. | n.a. | Coffee, banana |

Source: I.L.O., *Bulletin of Labour Statistics* (Geneva, 1975)

ding figures for Nigeria are 923,768 square kilometres and an estimated population of about 80 million, which is about 64.5 percent of the sub-region's total population. Generally, the countries of the region are poor and per capita GNP ranges from only $70 in Mali and Upper Volta to over $360 in Ivory Coast, but averages about $184.7 for the entire sub-region. Table I gives a profile of the region in terms of the membership of the ECOWAS, the estimated population, and the participation of the populations in agriculture and industry.

The ECOWAS states bring to the Community differing problems, colonial traditions and post-colonial experiences in development. The former French colonies of West Africa were closely knit economically, and even politically too, to the extent that French West Africa had a common currency, budget and tariff.[3] They had the advantage of geographical contiguity which encouraged mobility of persons. In contrast, the former British colonies never had, as a unit, strong economic relationship with the United Kingdom as the former French colonies had with France. Their trade links with Britain were individually organized. However, the British West African colonies had a common currency,[4] and loose economic co-operation in the form of common technical, research and commercial institutions. But these institutions which could have become the vehicle for post-independence economic co-operation were disbanded in the wake of economic and political nationalism that resulted in the unwillingness of these countries to surrender to, or share their newly-won independence with any supra-national authority. Furthermore, the English-speaking West African countries are divided by geography to the extent that none of them has common borders with each other.

## The ECOWAS Treaty

Previous attempts at the economic integration of West African States were limited by political and practical difficulties. This is not surprising for a region whose member countries had little to do with one another for nearly one century. Integration—and all kinds of integration—is a long-term task subject to the uncertainties that characterize most types of international co-operation. To expect spectacular results in the short or even medium-term is to be unrealistic.

The Treaty of ECOWAS was motivated by the recognition that external dependency is not an answer to development and the overriding need among member states to accelerate, foster and encourage the economic and social development of their states, thus improving the living standards of their peoples. The Treaty became a reality because of the commendable initiatives which the Heads of States of Nigeria and Togo took in 1972 and their determination to show through joint endeavours and co-operation that cooperation among West African countries is possible. The Treaty is also a tribute to the wisdom and positive response of West Africans to the political and economic needs of the region.

The Community aims at promoting co-operation and development in all fields of economic activity particularly in the fields of industry, transport, telecommunications, energy, agriculture, natural resources, commerce, monetary and financial questions and in social and cultural matters. It also aims at increasing and maintaining economic stability in member states by fostering closer relations among its members and thereby contributing to the progress and development of the African continent.

The Treaty is arranged under fourteen chapters, and consists of sixty-five articles. Its responsibility is delegated to five major institutions, namely the Authority of Heads of State and Government; the Council of Ministers; the Executive Secretariat; the Tribunal of the Community; and the Technical and Specialized Commissions. The Commissions handle trade, customs, immigration, monetary payments, industry, agriculture and natural resources and the social and cultural affairs.

The Treaty recognizes that various forms of bilateral and multilateral economic co-operation exist in the region and that this gives hope for a wider co-operation with fair and equitable distribution of benefits among member states. The ultimate objective is the sustained economic development of West Africa and the creation of homogeneous society leading to the unity of the region—a goal best and most quickly achieved by allowing complete free movement of goods, capital and, above all, people.

## Customs and Trade

It is anticipated that within fifteen years of the Treaty a customs union will be in full operation. The customs union will work towards the elimination of customs duties on imports and the relaxation of restrictions on trade among member states. This customs union is not a new experience in post-independence West Africa. Some of the French-speaking states have already gone through two such experiences, the UDEAO set up in 1959 and the CEAO which replaced it in 1973. But, at the same time, it must be stressed that these countries have not found it easy to co-operate even though they have a common colonial heritage.

The ECOWAS provisions are designed to increase trade between member states. Historically, the largest proportion of each member states' trade has been with countries outside Africa and there has been a very low level of inter-regional trade. Less than ten percent of total "official" West African trade is within the region itself. At the same time, there is considerable smuggling across the various national frontiers—although naturally no statistics are available on this. It is hoped that with the removal of trade barriers and the harmonization of trade and price policies smuggling can be eliminated.

ECOWAS member countries are allowed a period of two years to maintain present levels of duties. After the two year period and before the end of the eight year, members are required to progressively reduce and ultimately eliminate import duties in accordance with a schedule to be recommended to the Council of Ministers by the Trade, Custom, and Immigration, Monetary and Payments Commissions. This schedule will take into account the effects of the reduction and elimination of import duties on the revenue of member states and the need to avoid the disruption of the income they derive from import duties. This is not likely to be very substantial, since official trade between member states is small.

One particular trade provision that has recently been dealt a blow is that which declares that each member state, in accordance with international regulations shall grant full and unrestricted freedom of transit through its territory, to goods proceeding to or from a third country indirectly through that territory to or from other member states, and such transit shall not be subject to any discrimination, quantitative restrictions, duties or other charges levied on transit.

Not long after the ECOWAS Treaty was signed, Dahomey (now Benin) closed her borders with Togo and Nigeria—apparently on grounds of suspected political sabotage allegedly in Togo. The closure of the borders meant that Nigeria's goods delivered at Ghanaian ports and being transported through Togo and Benin could not get through. Togo viewed the situation as a deliberate attempt by Benin to prevent her Western neighbours from taking advantage of the port congestion in Lagos. Benin viewed it purely as a security measure. Whatever it was, the situation posed a serious threat to the fledgling ECOWAS and it epitomized some of the petty squabbles that have caused delay in establishing the Community and could continue to do so for some time.

## Industrial Development and Harmonization

West Africa, in an attempt to extricate herself from dependence on the export of unprocessed natural resources and agricultural produce—the major sources of foreign earnings—is busily engaged in rapid industrialization—at least for primary processing. The diversity of the region, with its unequal distribution of resources and varied economic and industrial policies, has prompted the Community to seek to harmonize member states' economic and industrial policies and to eliminate the disparities in the levels of development. This issue delayed the establishment of the Community. There are fears on the part of the comparatively less developed states of possible domination of the Community by the economically more powerful and developed countries in the region. Before any headway could be made it was of utmost importance that these fears be allayed.

The provisions for industrial development and harmonization fall in three stages:
1. an exchange of information on major industrial projects in member states to be supplied on request.
2. harmonization of industrial incentives and industrial development plans to ensure a similarity of industrial climate and to avoid disruption of their industrial activities resulting from dissimilar policies in the fields of industrial incentives, company taxation and Africanization, and also to avoid unhealthy rivalry, duplications and waste of resources, and
3. exchange of personnel and training, and the establishment of joint ventures.

It is hoped that by these arrangements, the technical efficiency of existing industrial projects will improve. They will, at least, be freed from restrictive tariff walls and directed towards a better utilization of resources within the member states.

## Co-operaton in Agriculture and Natural Resources

As with industrial development, the Community intends to harmonize agricultural projects and policies with the aim of achieving a common agricultural policy, paying particular attention to the fields of research, training, production, processing of products including, of course, the marketing of products of forestry, animal husbandry and fisheries. This aspect of the provisions of the Treaty should be taken very seriously since it is very important for the survival of the Community where all the member states are essentially agricultural, with a high proportion of the economically active population in this sector.

A common agricultural policy is important because most of the member states depend largely on agriculture for their foreign exchange.[5] Apart from the foreign exchange earning capacity of the agricultural sector, another reason for harmonizing agricultural policies is the fact that West African countries grow almost identical crops. They live in a region where similar geographical conditions run east-west while their political boundaries run north-south. A common policy for crops grown by more than one member-state is, therefore, essential.

## Monetary and Financial Matters

To achieve the proper supervision of the payments system within the Community, a committee of West African Central Banks has been set up. Prior to the ECOWAS, central banks in the West African sub-region had already established an association as part of the African wide Association of Central Banks and had also established a machinery for the multilateral settlement of payments so as to promote the use of each other's currencies for sub-regional trade and other transactions, to liberalize trade and to promote monetary co-operation. To aid the monetary machinery already set up, a West African Unit of Account is to be introduced in order to determine the conversion rates for various national currencies.

## Co-operation in Transport and Communications

Provision has been made in the Treaty for infrastructural links in the fields of transport and communications. Efficient transport communications are important in the success of the Community. This is so because until the establishment of the Community there have been few direct links between member states. A common transport policy would improve and expand existing links and aid the establishment of new ones. Such a process, no doubt, would enhance the physical cohesion of member states and promote greater mobility within the Community. The position now is that cables from English-speaking members to any of the neighbouring French-speaking members have to go through London and Paris. For this reason, the Community proposes to establish a direct, modern, efficient and rational system of telecommunications.

Mention may also be made of road systems which form the most important ingredient of the transport network in the region. Hitherto, there are few roads within the Community and even at the national level; the existing roads are unable to tap the resources of the various economies to the maximum, and there are very few all-weather roads. Railways seem to be in an even worse position.

Air transport is gaining popularity in the sub-region and almost all member states have airlines with scheduled landings at each other's ports. It is submitted that a Community airline could make air transport more efficient and more profitable besides standing international competition. Apart from harmonizing land and air transport, there should also be a plan for the harmonization and rationalization of policies on shipping and international waterways. The responsibility for this should be that of the Transport, Telecommunications and Energy Commission of the Community.[6]

## ECOWAS As a Weapon for Independence

There are sixteen[7] member states in ECOWAS and all but Cape Verde Islands are members of the high contracting parties. These high contracting parties accepted the need for a fair and equitable distribution of the benefits of co-operation. The four technical and specialized Commissions created by the Treaty perform the functions and act within the limits of the powers conferred upon them by or under the Treaty and Protocols of ECOWAS. Each Commission consists of representatives of member states, thus assuring equal access to decision-making and a fair share of the benefits.

## Benefits to be Derived by Citizens of Member States of the Community

It would seem to be accurate to state that all citizens of member states of ECOWAS are community citizens. Community citizens would feel quite at home in countries of other member states where efforts would be made to abolish all obstacles to their freedom of movement and residence. In fact, it has been strongly suggested that immigration laws of the member countries of the Community be scrapped.

Funds for the general operation of the Community are derived from various sources but the most direct is from annual contributions of member states. The amount to be paid by each member state, the form of payment and regulations governing such payments, are determined by the Council of Ministers. Other sources of funds are derived from incomes from Community enterprises, receipts from bilateral and multilateral sources as well as from subsidies and contributions from foreign sources. It would be disastrous for the Community to depend heavily on foreign sources as self-reliance must be maintained if the Community is to become an instrument for economic independence.

Regional integration is a process ultimately linked to the notion of a "Community." Basically, it may be seen as a way of achieving things. Okon Udokang asserts that the process of integration is a means of increasing the interaction and mingling of national units in order to obscure the boundaries between the system of international organizations and the environment provided by their nation state members.[8] Free movement of factors of production, including labour and capital, in a Community may generally result in efficiency. Factor mobility is important to the economic and political health of West Africa.

Perhaps one provision of the Treaty which, if properly applied, will turn the ECOWAS into an instrument for economic independence deals with customs union. An important purpose of the Community is to establish a customs union comprising all the countries in West Africa. Most of the analyses of the economic consequences of customs unions have been within the static frame-work. The main attention is focussed on the efficient distribution of existing output and better allocation of existing resources with a view to increasing the welfare of member countries. In short, the static effects relate to changes in trade flows that would follow reductions in duties under the assumption of unchanged production techniques. Apparently, a member of a customs union may gain from trade liberalization in respect of both exports and imports. But more generally, still within the static frame-work, the effects of a customs union are usually analyzed mainly in terms of trade creation and trade diversion. Trade creation arises as a result of reduction or elimination of tariff barriers against other countries since a member country now finds it profitable to import goods which it did not import before the union. Trade diversion would arise from the substitution of low-cost, foreign goods with high-cost goods produced by Community members. However, in the West African sub-region, these static effects, trade creation and trade diversion, may be of little significance. In fact, Helliener,[9] among others, has noted that the static analysis of the effects of a customs union, based mainly on the European experience, is of limited relevance to developing countries, who are desirous of achieving maximum rate of economic growth.

The dynamic effects of a customs union are those that result from a reallocation of resources and from changes in the structure of production due to the widening of national markets. Such effects comprise cost reductions or increased efficiency due to internal and external economies of scale and improvements in the methods of production that result from intensified foreign competition. Economies of scale in research and foreign competition tend to encourage technological advancement thereby accelerating economic growth. Furthermore, the broadening of the market to include all the member states of the ECOWAS will provide outlets for goods and services of these countries thereby encouraging producers to expand production. One may agree with Balassa that economic integration usually results in significant internal and external economies of scale, and he cited some studies that indicate a positive correlation between market size and output per head.[10] However, some economists have argued that economic integration could lead to only minor gains from economies of scale.[11] But the truth appears to be that the idea of economic integration is generally motivated by the desire for economies of scale and in West Africa it cannot be divorced from the problems of dependency and the need for regional self-reliance.

## Conclusion

ECOWAS has been described as a challenging experience in that it would enable the countries of West African sub-region to come to grips with some of the extensive and formidable problems of development. It is an exciting and challenging experience for the members of the Community to compare their current development experiences, share with each other the dimensions of their problems and evolve and agree upon common strategies to achieve economic, political and cultural independence. In this context, it is reassuring for the Nigerian Head of State, Lieutenant-General Olusegun Obasanjo, to assert that the ECOWAS treaty "was now leading to the desired goals of the economic upbringing of Africa."[12] However, a note of warning may be sounded. If ECOWAS is really to fulfill the hopes and aspirations of its founding fathers, the Community must learn from the bitter experiences of the East African Community (EAC). Firstly, there is the need for member countries to surrender some measure of their sovereignty to the Community. The East African Community collapsed because the political will could not be sustained. In fact, the methods and procedures of industrial allocation were often a matter of political bargaining in which no party was willing to yield ground. Secondly, the only mechanism provided for the distribution of industrial activities—the Industrial Licensing Acts—had several deficiencies. Before the EAC Treaty was signed the industrial licensing system had long been believed to have resulted in unbalanced industrial development in favour of Kenya and there was no sensitive machinery for overcoming this shortcoming. It is our view that ECOWAS can be transformed into an instrument of economic independence in West African sub-region provided that the human or structural problems are not found insurmountable and that the political will to maintain regional independence in West Africa is strong.

## BIBLIOGRAPHY

BALASSA, BOLA. *Trade Liberalization Among Industrial Countries: Objectives and Alternatives.* New York: McGraw-Hill Corp., 1967.

CLEMENT, M. O., et al. *Theoretical Issues in International Economics.* New York: Houghton Mifflin Corp., 1967.

ECOWAS. *The Treaty of the Economic Community of West African States.* Lagos, 1976.

HELLIENER, GERALD K. "Nigeria and the African Common Market." *The Nigerian Journal of Economic and Social Studies.* 4 (1962).

I.L.O. *Bulletin of Labour Statistics.* Geneva, 1975.

OKWUOSA, EMMANUEL. *New Direction for Economic Development in Africa.* London: Africa Books, 1976.

ONITIRI, H. M. A. "Towards a West African Economic Community." *The Nigerian Journal of Economic and Social Studies.* 5 (1963).

UDOKANG, OKON. "ECOWAS and Problems of Regional Integration." *Times International,* 1976.

## NOTES

1 Emmanuel Okwuosa, *New Direction for Economic Development in Africa* (London, 1976), p. 80.
2 Mallam Adamu Ciroma, Opening Address during the Joint Conference by Nigerian Institute of International Affairs and Central Bank of Nigeria on ECOWAS, 23-27 August 1976.
3 H. M. A. Onitiri, "Towards a West African Economic Community," *The Nigerian Journal of Economic and Social Studies,* vol. 5, no. 1 (1963), pp. 27-30.

4   The four West African Sterling area countries of Nigeria, Gold Coast (Ghana) Sierra Leone and the Gambia had a common currency, the West African pound, issued by the West African Currency Board which was established in 1912. In the late 1950s and early 1960s, each of the countries established its own national currency thus ending the half a century experience of a unified monetary authority.

5   Nigeria has become the only exception because of her petroleum resources.

6   See: *West Africa* (31 October 1977) for details of an agreement signed at ECOWAS Lagos headquarters under which the U.N. Economic Commission for Africa (ECA) will carry out, on behalf of ECOWAS, studies on the development of transport and telecommunications system within the sixteen states of the community. The funds which amount to some $250,000 will be provided by ECOWAS.

7   Cape Verde Islands joined later after its independence from Portugal on 5 July 1975. [Editor: The paper was written before many of the provisions of the Treaty were implemented.]

8   Okon Udokang, "ECOWAS and Problem of Regional Integration," *Times International* (22 March 1976).

9   Gerald K. Helliener, "Nigeria and the African Common Market," *The Nigerian Journal of Economic and Social Studies,* vol. 4, no. 3 (1962), p. 293.

10  Balassa, *Liberalization among Industrial Countries,* New York, 1967, p. 98-9.

11  For discussion on this topic see M. O. Clement, et al., *Theoretical Issues in International Economics* (New York: Houghton Mifflin Corp., 1967), p. 200.

12  *New Nigerian* (22 April 78).

# The Indigenisation
# of "Imported Religions"

*How Independent are our Religious Ideas?*

E. ILOGU

*Teachers' Service Commission, Anambra State, Enugu, Nigeria*

A FEW WORDS IN THE TITLE of this paper—"indigenisation", "imported religions", "independent religious ideas"—require some interpretation or clarification. The effort to express the Christian religion in the African cultural idioms, made necessary by political developments and the growing demand for mutual cultural respect which was hastened by World War II, led the drive to indigenisation. Indigenisation literally means "to make native", "to adapt to a given area", "to acclimatize or to habituate to a new climate, a new cultural environment or milieu". Indigenisation, therefore, could be understood in this paper to apply to the creative activities in verbalization, articulation in music, drama or art, and the explanation of a religion received from outside as part of the way of life of the receiving people.

In the context of the West African peoples, two religions have come from outside, namely, Christianity and Islam. Because, historically, these two religions started, developed and were introduced into West Africa from Europe and the Middle East, areas whose cultures contrasted with those in West Africa, these religions have come to be known as imported religions. Maybe a more expressive phrase could be "exported religions" since West Africa did not place an "order" for these religions. The "imported religions", Islam and Christianity, carry with them cultural values, concepts and world views which are foreign to West Africa. Of these two religions, Christianity will be singled out as the focal point of the study.

The reality of existence indicates that no entity, idea, person or social unit is absolutely "separate from" or "self-sufficient" or "self-consistent"—some of the meanings attached to the word "independent". In this context, I suggest that independence of our religious ideas is possible as well as impossible; it is realisable as well as utopian. Ideas are concepts, view points, systems of values or vehicles for conveying meanings by which a dialogue or communication takes place between persons. Religion is more difficult to define. It is often used as coterminous with faith, systems of belief and practices which result from them, cults, relationship between the human and the supernatural, theologies or views about gods and God. Remember that some investigators have collected scores of definitions of religion and finally rejected all of them in their attempt to find, from their point of view, a more satisfactory one. For my part, and in this paper, religion means the Christian religion; and "religious ideas" are concepts, values and meanings resulting from the teaching and the practice of the Christian Faith.

With such narrowing down of the areas and the standpoints of our discussion, we can proceed to the examination of the subject matter of this paper.

## Background to Indigenisation of Christianity in West Africa

A quick look at the literature dealing with Christianity and cultural change will set the stage. Writers in the last decade or two have approached the theme of Christianity and cultural change in Africa from many angles. Historians, social anthropologists and novelists can be easily named among such writers. In his *Missionary Factors in East Africa,* Roland Oliver did not only trace the history of the development of Christianity in East Africa, but analysed some aspects of social and cultural changes brought into the area by the coming of Christianity.[1] This pattern of historical writing was followed by Nigerian historians like Jacob Ajayi,[2] Emmanuel Ayandele,[3] Felix Ekechi,[4] and Elizabeth Isichei.[5]

Significantly enough, Professor Ajayi's *Christian Missions in Nigeria* is subtitled "the making of a new elite", indicating the seriousness with which he viewed Christianity as a social catalyst bringing about cultural change that led to the emergence of a new class of Nigerians. The word "elite" immediately suggests some class of people who have "outgrown" an existing cultural milieu and have entered into some new pattern of culture that is either in the making or is already made. These historians emphasized a common theme, the arrival and growth of Christianity in Africa, and its role as an agent of cultural change, a line of historiography that assumed a good proportion of space in the academic handling of African studies both in Africa and elsewhere.

Social anthropologists have also emphasized cultural change in their "impact studies". Monica Wilson[6] is a case in point. She raises some of the questions which the Nyakyusa of Tanzania or the Ndembu of Zambia would ask about their cultural roots now that they have converted to Christianity. Christianity has brought about increase in social scale and also freedom of choice. A major aspect of the cultural change brought about by Christianity to Central Africa was that many people have found the choices open to them almost overwhelming. We all know that choice-making, in a fast changing society, can disrupt people. This is one aspect of cultural change brought about by Christianity in Africa which many social anthropologists point out. Field reports indicate how a religious response to Jehovah's Witnesses, a Christian sect, gives rise not only to social change in a Zambian rural community but also helps to raise a new crop of individuals disciplined in new occupations like farm management, shop keeping, brick laying and responsible cooperative endeavours. The cultural change advocated by this sect is traumatic and dichotomous. A member of the sect is required to cut off all traditional kinship ties and duties as these are regarded as inconsistent with the ethos of being a Jehovah's Witness. This pattern of disruption in culture is also noticeable in the early conversions to orthodox Christianity among the Igbo of Nigeria.[7]

African novelists have made the theme of cultural disruption and political protest their major concern. In *Things Fall Apart*, Achebe,[8] the distinguished Nigerian novelist, describes the inability of the centre to hold together owing to the disruption of the village life partly brought about by the school education and the local church. Nwoye, the son of Okonkwo, is the hero of the novel. The thought of Nwoye becoming a Christian made Okonkwo mad. He argued that if all his male children became Christians like Nwoye he would face annihilation in the spirit world of the ancestors for no one would give the ancestors any more worship and sacrifice. To Okonkwo things were surely "falling apart" due to the activities of Mr. Kinga, the evangelist at Mbanta, and his white missionaries at Umuofia. In *No Longer At Ease*, it is another tale of disruption in Igbo cultural patterns brought about by Christians like Obi who would attempt to marry an *osu* girl, a cult slave, a marriage forbidden by the earth deity. James Ngugi in *The River Between* criticises the Christian religion because it took no account of the African way of life: "...a religion that did not recognise spots of beauty and truth in their way of life was useless. It would not satisfy. It would not be a living experience, a source of life and vitality. It would only maim a man's soul."[9] In their approach to social change in Africa resulting from the planting of Christianity in the continent, African novelists emphasize discontinuity of culture as they paint a portrait of a people who are torn between their loyalty to the old community of kith and kin and the new community built around the church and its membership of which they are a part.

## Process of Indigenisation

The conflict between African traditional institutions and the imported religions, particularly Christianity, has made indigenisation a practical necessity. We will illustrate this process by considering two areas—the Akan of Ghana and the Igbo of Nigeria.

### The Akan of Ghana

The Akan people inhabit most of the southern half of Ghana. They trace descent matrilineally and speak a more or less common language with dialectical variations. They share a common pattern of political, economic, social and religious institutions.

The Portuguese landed on Akan land in 1482. The Christian faith dates from this period but the modern missionary work started a little more than one hundred years ago. The principal Church units are the Roman Catholic, the Presbyterian, the Methodist and the Anglican; and some prophet movement churches have also emerged. Two major themes need emphasis in a study of the influences of Christianity on the cultural life of the Akan: the tension between Akan and Christian understanding of the values and the intentions of *rites de passage;* and how Akan cultural and social structures have adapted to some patterns of church life and organisation.

Akan rites of passage include the usual birth and naming ceremony, puberty, marriage and burial. On the eighth day an Akan infant undergoes the naming ceremony, usually performed by the head of the family, who formally incorporates the infant into the lineage. The Church has neglected this ceremony in preference to its practice of infant baptism. This has sometimes, in the recent past, disrupted the family and lineage link because children who did not receive the naming ceremony are not regarded as fully incorporated into the lineage. To avoid this ambiguous situation, some Christian parents perform the traditional naming ceremony as well as the infant baptism. Many girls have now abandoned the actual puberty rites in preference for Christian confirmation to which they incorporate the social aspects of the Akan puberty rites—the wearning of fine clothes, and parading in them for some days (on which such girls take holidays from work), receiving of traditional gifts and feasting of friends and age mates. Just as puberty rite was a preparation for marriage in traditional Akan society so has the confirmation.

Akan marriage has always been an affair of two families. The Christian Church has tried almost in vain to introduce the Western concept of marriage as an affair of the two couples and their family life a monogamous one with ultimate relation ''and mutual responsibility of husband and wife towards each other and towards their children as a closed group which admits no interference from without.'' As a contract between two families Akan marriage allows the husband and the wife to retain primary loyalties to their respective kinship group. Interference from any of such group is part of the marriage contract. A Christian couple trying to obey both the demands of their Akan tradition as well as the teachings of the Western missionary or his Ghanaian successor will experience much conflict in their family life. To lessen or completely do away with such conflict Akan Christians are developing a new marriage ethos which combines the two traditions—Christian and Akan. Sometimes this combination may involve a male Christian in a polygamous situation. The principal features, however, are Native customary Law combined with Ordinance Marriage Law; loyalty to respective kinship group coupled with loyalty between the spouses; matrilineal inheritance coupled with father-care for the children; the care and nurture of the children in the Christian faith by the Christian parents coupled with their education in the traditional pattern which the extended family and members of the maternal lineage owe to the children. The modification of the Akan way of life by the Christian presence and the differences between the Akan Christian family life and the Christian family in Europe are clear enough.

The last of the rites of passage we will consider is the burial ceremony. Busia's study is worth citing:

> A long procession headed by a choir and a priest may wend its way to the cemetery to bury the dead according to Christian rites; but this is followed by traditional rites. For example at dead of night, another procession, expressing very different beliefs, may follow the widower

who carries live coal to the sea-shore for a ceremonial bath to chase away evil spirits. The widower, who may be literate or illiterate, goes through a series of other rites and taboos to avert misfortunes. The sacrifice of a sheep to the dead may be followed by a 'wake-keeping' when mourners sit up all night singing Christian hymns; but next morning libations are poured to the dead, and donations received according to custom. The following Sunday, the relatives of the deceased attend a Thanksgiving Service, sometimes all clad in the same type of cloth, to hear prayers said, and listen to consoling exhortations based on Christian beliefs; but a day or two later there may be drumming and dancing in the traditional style of mourning.[10]

This quotation shows us that the Akan insist on being Akans as well as Christians in the way a British Missionary would wish. Busia did say that in some of these ceremonies different groups take part in different activities at the same time. But the essential point to take note of is the continued desire of the people to show that it is not different units of Akan society—Christian and non-Christian—burying the dead. Rather it is the one Akan people acting together as the community built already by their ancestors.

When we look at the organisation of the administrative and the pastoral or ecclesiastical structures of the Presbyterian and the Methodist Churches, for example, we see how closely related these structure are to the traditional Akan society structures. Here let me quote the words of S.G. Williamson as they very amply illustrate the point I am trying to make here:

Ministers, catechists, and elders, with the members, reflect the Akan structure of a chief, linguists, elders, and commoners, the minister occupying a position analogous to that of the chief, the catechist that of linguist, the elders that of State elders, each grade exercising closely resembling responsibilities. The supreme court of the local church is the pastor with his session (Presbyterian) or the minister with his leaders (Methodist) exercising a function similar to that of the chief in council. The affairs of the central church and its sub-stations are overlooked by this central court which undertakes responsibility for the administration, business and financial, and the over-sight of the spiritual welfare of the congregations—the court is omnicompetent. A substantial proportion of the time of ministers and elders is absorbed in the hearing of 'cases'; they act as a tribunal to which members, singly or in groups, bring their affairs for settlement. Quarrels, disagreements, wrong-doing of all kinds come to them. The local church, with its sub-stations, is an imperium set within the wider Akan society.[11]

We can see in this aspect of Christianity and social change in Africa the Troeltsch model of the influence of existing social structures, cultural patterns and historical situations upon the growth of a Church. Suffice it is now to end this brief review of Christianity and the Akan people with this curious fact that the missionaries in the Akan area translated the word "ordained minister" or "priest" into the Akan word "*Osofo*"—the same word used for the officiating priest at the traditional shrine of Akan gods. This borrowing by the Christian Church shows that cultural exchange is not unidirectional.

### The Igbo of Nigeria

Brief mention of examples of indigenisation in Igboland will be made. Public worship has borrowed from traditional Igbo hymn tunes, drumming instruments, as well as hand clapping and dance posturing. The second burial ceremonies for deceased *Ozo* title holders were denounced by missionaries but have become institutionalized in most Christian churches in the form of memorial services. *Ozo* title taking is now approved by the Roman Catholic Church and christening with Igbo names has become the rule rather than the taboo it was in the first two decades of this century. Many Christian theologians and sociologists now boldly recommend to the Church authorities the necessity of Christianizing institutions like tribute giving (*ife-nru*), all aspects of *ozo* title taking and polygyny.[12]

Through all these examples of and attempts at indigenisation, religious ideas are enlarged, clarified and sometimes are more confused. Take the idea of Christian family life in the light of the practice of polygyny. The narrow mission policy handed to Nigerian Christians some sixty years ago will surely receive a rude shock when a strict and narrow Biblical interpretation is used to show that possibly a baptised Christian who is faithful to his two legitimate wives might remain within Divine Grace whilst the baptised Christian monogamist may not, depending upon behaviour. Common participation by all the members of a given village in the burial of a Christian is bound to alter the idea of the Christian fellowship. When puberty is associated with confirmation in the Church, the religious ideas associated with maturity in the Faith is bound to be viewed from a wider perspective. When an *Ozo* title holder receives sacralization of life through the initiation of older title holders and the laying on of hands by a priest together with the prayers of fellow Christians, sacralization of life for such a Christian *ozo* title will no doubt acquire wider meaning. There is no doubt, therefore, that Christian religious ideas in the context of indigenisation will be different from the ideas "imported" from Europe. This does not necessarily mean that under indigenisation Christian religious ideas in West Africa will be completely independent of such identical religious ideas among Christians in Europe, America or elsewhere.

### The Nature of Religious Ideas

Preliminary consideration about religious ideas should take note of the existence of literal and figurative use of words. When I say "God is holy," I am using "God" and "holy" literally, but when I say "Mao Tse-Tung is the god of the Chinese," I am using "god" analogically. Such figurative and literal use of words in religious language makes religious ideas sometimes difficult to grasp, analyse and communicate to others. Secondly, a great deal of religious activities is symbolic, therefore the ideas they contain elude scientific analysis. Thirdly, religious ideas like many other ideas are time bound and therefore express concepts, world views and the "sciences" of ages gone by into which present thought forms do not easily penetrate. This is to suggest that there are some nagging problems besetting precise analysis of religious ideas. These problems notwithstanding, some attempt at analysing the nature of religious ideas will now be made so as to indicate how the question "How independent are our religious ideas" can be answered.

Religious ideas can be grouped into three—cognitive, affirmative and descriptive. Cognitive religious ideas stress the areas of religious knowledge discernible by the activity of the mind. Such ideas are capable of logical processes and fit into what could be called scientific-matter-of-fact ideas. Religious ideas like justice, mercy and love are simple examples. Acts of justice or mercy or love can be quantified and they are ideas which do have "wings" to travel far and wide and start revolutions and changes in societies. Cognitive processes can also be applied in the conceptualizations generated by religion which include statements of religious history, religious artefacts and religious organizations.

Affirmative religious ideas are those which repeat and affirm what religionists believe in and possibly practise. Such ideas can be expressed in creeds, confessionals and statements of faith. Such ideas may not be put into logical conclusions but give satisfaction to those who hold and purvey them.

Descriptive religious ideas are applied to describe religious concepts which are usually unseen and therefore cannot be physically handled. Such descriptions are applied to God, Eternal Life, Angels and other "bodies" found in religion. Every religion has its religious ideas which can be analyzed under these categories.

## Conclusion

The question can now be put: "How independent are our religious ideas?" We have discussed the attempts at indigenisation of the Christian Church in West Africa. Such indigenisation is meant to facilitate the inclusion of our cultural heritage and experience into the expression, teaching and the localization of the Christian Faith. When the process of indigenisation is completed, if ever it will, the religious ideas of West African Christians can never become completely independent. Human beings have a common ideational heritage which makes it possible for an idea expressed in one language to be interpreted in or communicated to another language. Love is love everywhere even when the mode of expressing love differs. Therefore, no amount of indigenisation of the Christian Church can make us completely independent of other units of humanity in our religious ideas.

### BIBLIOGRAPHY

ACHEBE, CHINUA. *No Longer At Ease*. London, 1960.
——. *Things Fall Apart*. London: Heinemann, 1958.
AJAYI, J. *Christian Missions in Nigeria 1814-1891*. London: Longmans, 1964.
AYANDELE, E. *The Missionary Impact on Modern Nigeria 1842-1914*. London: Longmans, 1966.
BUSIA, K. A. *A Social Survey of Sekondi-Takoradi*. London: Crown Agents, 1950.
EKECHI, F. K. *Missionary Enterprise and Rivalry in Igboland 1857-1914*. London: Frank Cass, 1972.
ILOGU, E. *Christianity and Ibo Culture*. Leiden: E. J. Brill, 1974.
ISICHEI, E. *The Ibo People and the Europeans*. London: Faber and Faber, 1973.
NGUGI, W. *The River Between*. London, 1967.

OLIVER, R. *Missionary Factor in East Africa.* London: Longmans, 1952.
WILLIAMSON, S. G. *Akan Religion and the Christian Faith.* Accra: Ghana University Press, 1965.
WILSON, M. *Religion and the Transformation of Society: A Study in Social Change in Africa.* Cambridge: University Press, 1971.

## NOTES

1  Oliver, *Missionary Factors in East Africa,* London, Longmans, 1952.
2  Ajayi, Christian Missions in Nigeria, 1814-1891, London, Longmans, 1964.
3  Ayandele, *The Missionary Impact on Modern Nigeria, 1842-1914,* London, Longmans, 1966.
4  Ekechi, *Missionary Enterprise and Rivalry in Igboland, 1857-1914,* London, Frank Cass, 1972.
5  Isichei, *The Ibo People and the Europeans,* London, Faber and Faber, 1973.
6  Wilson, *Religion and the Transformation of Society—A Study in Social Change in Africa,* Cambridge University Press, 1971.
7  Ilogu, *Christianity and Ibo Culture,* Leiden, E. J. Brill, 1974, pp. 63-75.
8  Achebe, *Things Fall Apart,* London, Heinemann, 1958; *No Longer At Ease,* London, 1960.
9  Ngugi, *The River Between,* London, 1967.
10  Busia, *A Social Survey of Sekondi-Takoradi,* London, Crown Agents, 1950.
11  Williamson, *Akan Religion and the Christian Faith,* Accra, Ghana Universities Press, 1965.
12  Ilogu, *Christianity and Igbo Culture,* Leiden, E. J. Brill, 1974, pp. 215-228.

# SELECTED BIBLIOGRAPHY

AMIN, SAMIR. *Accumulation on a World Scale: A Critique of the Theory of Underdevelopment.* New York: Monthly Review Press, 1974.
——. *Neocolonialism in West Africa.* Penguin African Library, 1973.
——. *Unequal Development.* Sussex, England, 1976.
AWA, EME. "The Place of Ideology in Nigerian Politics." *African Review* 4 (1974): 358-364.
BALASSA, BOLA. *Trade Liberalization Among Industrial Countries: Objectives and Alternatives.* New York: McGraw-Hill Corp., 1967.
BARAN, P. A. and SWEEZY, P. M. *Monopoly Capital.* England: Penguin, 1960.
BARAN, PAUL A. *The Political Economy of Growth.* London: Modern Reader Paperbacks, 1958.
BARNET, R. J. and MULLER, R. E. *Global Reach: The Power of Multinational Corporations.* New York, 1974.
BATH, RICHARD C. and JAMES, D. D. "Dependency Analysis of Latin America: Some Criticisms, Some Suggestions." *Latin American Research Review* 11 (1976): 3-53.
BAUER, P. T. *West African Trade: A Study of Competition, Oligopoly and Monopoly in a Changing Economy.* London: Routledge and K. Paul, 1963.
BECKFORD, GEORGE L. *Persistent Poverty: Underdevelopment in Plantation Economies of the Third World.* London: Oxford University Press, 1972.
BENDIX, R. *Nation Building and Citizenship.* New York, 1964.
BONAPARTE, T. H. "Multi-national Corporations and Culture in Liberia." *The American Journal of Economics and Sociology* 38 (1979): 237-51.
BOULDING, KENNETH E. *The Impact of Social Sciences.* Rutgers University Press, 1966.
BRENNER, R. "The Origin of Capitalist Development: Critique of Neo-Smithian Marxism." *New Left Review* 104 (1977): 25-92.
BRETT, E. A. *Colonialism and Underdevelopment in East Africa: The Politics of Economic Change 1919-1939.* New York: Nok Publishers, 1973.
BROKKFILED, HAROLD. *Interdependent Development.* London: Methuen and Co., 1975.
BROWN, BARRAT. *The Economics of Imperialism.* Penguin, 1974.
CARDOSO, FERNANDO H. "The Consumption of Dependency Theory in the United States." *Latin American Research Review* XII, 3 (1977): 7-24.
——. "Dependency and Development in Latin America." *New Left Review* 74 (July-August 1972).
CHENERY, HOLLIS B. "The Structural Approach to Development Policy." *American Economic Review* LXV (1975): 301-16.
CHENERY, HOLLIS, B., et al. *Redistribution With Growth.* Published for the World Bank by Oxford University Press, 1974.
CHILCOTE, RONALD H. "Dependency: A Critical Synthesis of the Literature." *Latin American Perspectives* I, 1 (1974): 4-27.
——. "A Question of Dependency." *Latin American Research Review* XII, 2 (1978): 55-68.
CHODAK, S. *Societal Development (Five Approaches).* New York: Oxford University Press, 1973.
CLEMENT, M. O., et al. *Theoretical Issues in International Economics.* New York: Houghton Mifflin Corp., 1967.
ELIAS, T. O., et al., eds. *African Indigenous Laws.* Enugu: Government Printer, 1975.
FAGAN, R. R. "Cuban Revolutionary Politics." *Monthly Review* 23 (1972).
FERNÁNDEZ, RAÚL A. and OCAMPO, JOSÉ F. "The Latin American Revolution: A Theory of Imperialism, Not Dependence." *Latin American Perspectives* I, 1 (1974): 30-61.
FRANK, A. G. *Capitalism and Underdevelopment in Latin America.* New York: Monthly Review Press, 1969.
——. "The Development of Underdevelopment." In *Imperialism and Underdevelopment: A Reader.* Edited by R. I. Rhodes. New York: Monthly Review Press, 1970.
——. *Latin America: Underdevelopment or Revolution?* New York, 1969.
——. *Lumpenbourgeoisie: Lumpendevelopment: Dependence, Class and Politics in Latin America.* New York: Monthly Review Press, 1972.

FRANK, GUNDER. "Dependence is Dead, Long Live Dependence and Class Struggle: A Reply to Critics." *Latin American Perspectives* I, 1 (1974): 87-106.

GALTUNG, JOHAN, "A Structural Theory of Imperialism." *The African Review* I (1972-1973): 93-138.

——. "A Structural Theory of Imperialism." *Journal of Peace Research*, 1971, pp. 81-118.

GEERTZ, GLIFFORD. *The Interpretation of Cultures.* London: Hutchinson, 1975.

GILBERT, GUY J. "Socialism and Dependency." *Latin American Perspectives* I, 1 (1974): 107-23.

HAILEY, LORD. *An African Survey.* London: Oxford University Press, 1956 edition.

HARRIS, RICHARD, ed. *The Political Economy of Africa.* Cambridge, Mass., 1975.

HEGEL, G. W. F. *Science of Logic.* Translated by A. V. Miller. London: George Allen and Urwin Ltd., 1969.

HOPKINS, A. G. "Clio-Antics: A Horoscope for African Economic History." In *African Studies Since 1945: A Tribute to Basil Davidson.* Edited by C. Fyfe. London: Longmans, 1976.

——. *An Economic History of West Africa.* New York, 1973.

KARAM, A. E. "The Meaning of Dependence." *The Developing Economies* XIV 3 (1976): 201-211.

KARSH, B. and COLE, E. "Industrialization and the Convergence Hypothesis: Some Aspects of Contemporary Japan." *Journal of Social Issues* XXIV (1968): 45-64.

LAGOS, GUSTAVO. *International Stratification and Underdeveloped Countries.* Chapel Hill, 1963.

LANGER, SUSAN K. *Philosophy in a New Key: A Study in the Symbolism of Reason, Rite and Art.* New York: Mentor Books, 1962.

LEWIS, W. A. "Economic Development with Unlimited Supplies of Labour." *The Manchester School* 22 (1954): 139-191.

MACBEAN, A. I. "The Short-term Consequences of Export Instability." In *Economic Policy for Development.* Edited by I. Livingstone. Penguin, 1977.

MAFEJE, A. "The Fallacy of Dual Economies." *East Africa Journal*, 1972, pp. 7-9.

——. "The Fallacy of Dual Economies Revisited." In *Dualism and Rural Development in East Africa.* Edited by P. Kongstad. Copenhagen: Institute for Development Research, Denmark, 1973.

MAGDOFF, HARRY. "Imperialism Without Colonies." In *Studies in the Theory of Imperialism.* Edited by R. Owen and Bod Sutcliff. London: Longmans, 1972.

MARX, KARL. Capital, vol. I. Translated by Samuel Moore and Edward Aveling. Budapest, 1976.

MEYER, G. G. "Theories of Convergence." In *Changes in Communist Systems.* Edited by C. Johnson. Stanford University Press, 1965.

MORAWETZ, DAVID. *Twenty-five Years of Economic Development: 1950 to 1975.* Baltimore: The Johns Hopkins University Press, 1977.

MUNRO, J. FORBES. *Africa and the International Economy, 1800-1960.* London, 1976.

MYINT, HLA. "The 'Classical Theory' of International Trade and the Underdeveloped Countries." *Economic Journal* LXVIII (20): 317-37.

MYRDAL, GUNNAR. *Asian Drama: An Inquiry Into the Poverty of Nations.* New York: Twentieth Century fund, 1968.

——. *Rich Lands and Poor Lands: The Road to World Prosperity.* New York: Harper, 1957.

NKRUMAH, KWAME. *Neo-Colonialism, the Last Stage of Imperialism.* New York, 1965.

O'BRIEN, PHILIP, J. "A Critique of Latin American Theories of Dependency." In *Beyond the Sociology of Development: Economy and Society in Latin American and Africa.* Edited by Iva Oxaal, et al. London: Routledge and Kegan Paul, 1975, pp. 7-27.

OKWUOSA, EMMANUEL. *New Direction for Economic Development in Africa.* London: Africa Books, 1976.

ONI, COMRADE OLA and ONIMODE, BADE. *Economic Development of Nigeria, The Socialist Alternative.* Ibadan: The Nigerian Academy of Arts, Sciences and Technology, 1975.

ONYECHI, J. N. M. "A Problem of Assimilation or Dominance?" *African Indigenous Laws.* Edited by T. O. Elias, et al. Enugu, 1975.

PERHAM, MARGERY. *Colonial Sequence 1930-1949.* London: Methuen, 1967.

——, ed. *Mining, Commerce, and Finance in Nigeria.* London, 1948.

PINTO, A and KNAKAL, J. "The Centre-Periphery System Twenty Years Later." *Social and Economic Studies* 22 (1973): 64-70.

PREBISCH, R. *The Economics of Development of Latin America and Its Problems.* New York: U.N. Department of Social and Economic Affairs, 1960.

RAY, DAVID. "The Dependency Model of Latin-American Under-Development: Three Basic Fallacies." *Journal of Inter-American and World Affairs* XV, 1 (1973): 4-20.

RESNIK, S. A. "State of Development Economics." *American Economic Review* LXV (1975): 317-22.

RIESMAN, DAVID. *Abundance For What?* New York: Doubleday and Company, Inc., 1964.

RITLER, A. R. M. "Growth, Strategy and Economic Performance in Revolutionary Cuba: Past, Present and Prospective." *Social and Economic Studies* 21 (1972): 313-37.

ROBINSON, JOAN. "Michal Kalecki on the Economics of Capitalism." *Oxford Bulletin of Economics and Statistics* 39 (1977): 7-17.

RODNEY, W. *How Europe Underdeveloped Africa.* Dar-es-Salaam: Tanzania Publishing House, 1973.

ROSTOW, W. W. *The Stages of Economic Growth: A Non-Communist Manifesto.* Cambridge University Press, 1960.

SANTOS, THEOTONIO DOS. "The Structure of Dependence." *American Economic Review* LX (1970): 231-36.

SEARS. D., ed. *Cuba: The Economic and Social Revolution.* North Carolina University Press, 1964.

SINGER, H. W. "Dualism Revisited: A New Approach to the Problems of Dual Society in Developing Countries." *Journal of Development Studies* VII (1970).

SMITH, ADAM. *The Wealth of Nations: An Inquiry Into the Nature and Causes.* New York: The Modern Library, 1937.

SUTCLIFF, R. B. *Industry and Underdevelopment.* London: Addison-Wesley, 1971.

SZENTES, TAMAS. *The Political Economy of Underdevelopment.* Budapest: Akademiaikia, 1973.

TODARO, M. P. *Economic Development in the Third World.* London: Longmans, 1977.

UCHENDU, V. C. "The Challenge of Cultural Transitions in Sub-Saharan Africa." *The ANNALS—American Academy of Political and Social Sciences* 432 (1977): 70-9.

UDOKANG, OKON. "ECOWAS and Problems of Regional Integration." *Times International,* 1976.

VEBLEN, T. *The Impact of Workmanship and the State of Industrial Arts.* New York: Macmillan, 1914.

WALLERSTEIN, I. "Dependence in an Interdependent World: The Limited Possibilities of Transformation within the Capitalist World Economy." *African Studies Review* XVII (1974): 1-27.

———. *The Origins of the Modern World Systems.* New York, 1974.

WILES, P. "Will Capitalism and Communism Spontaneously Converge?" *ENCOUNTER* XXI (1963): 84-90.

WODDIS, JACK. *Introduction to Neo-Colonialism: The New Imperialism in Asia, Africa and Latin America.* New York: International Publishers, 1967.

WORSLEY, PETER. *The Third World.* London, 1964.

# CONTRIBUTORS

J. C. Aghaji is a practising Barrister-at-law in Enugu, Anambra State, Nigeria. A doctoral candidate in Political Science at the University of Nigeria, Nsukka, Mr. Aghaji holds the LL. M. degree of the University of London. He was formerly a Research Fellow in the Institute of African Studies, University of Nigeria, Nsukka.

S. J. S. Cookey is Professor of History and Head, Africana Studies Department, Rutger's University, New Brunswick, New Jersey. A graduate of the University of London where he earned his Ph.D., Professor Cookey is the author of two books: *Britain and the Congo Question 1885-1913* (Longman, London: 1968); and *King Jaja of the Niger Delta: His Life and Times 1821-91* (New York: NOK: 1974).

Rev. Canon E. C. U. Ilogu is the Chairman, Public Service Commission, Anambra State, Nigeria. A professor emeritus in Religion and Philosophy at the University of Nigeria, Nsukka, where he served as the Head, Department of Religion and Dean of the Faculty of Social Sciences, the Rev. Canon Professor E. C. U. Ilogu is the author of three books: *Christianity and Igbo Culture* (Leiden: 1974), *Social Philsophy for the Nigerian Nation* (Onitsha: 1962), and *West Meets East: A Report of Visit to East Africa* (London: 1955). Professor Ilogu holds a Ph.D. from the University of Leiden in the Netherlands.

Samuel Kodjo is Professor of Economics and Dean of the Faculty of Social Sciences at the University of Nigeria, Nsukka. Professor Kodjo holds Dr. habititatus (Venia Legendi) and is the author of the following works: *Bildungsplanung in Afrika suedlich der Sahara unter besonderer Buruecksichtigung des Universitae sunterrichts in den Wirtschafts- und Sozialwissenschaften. Ein Beitrag zur Bildungsoekonomik*, Cologne, 1968; *Probleme de Akkulturation in Afria Die entwicklungspolitischen Auswirkungen Moderner Schulausbildung und Kommunikationsmedien*, Meisenneim on the Glan, 1973; and with Wolfgang Arnold and Ernst-Albrecht von Renesse *Qualitativer Bedarf der Entwicklungslaender in der Zweiten Entwicklungsdekade in den Bereichen: Bildung, Wissenschaft und Technologie, Boehum 1972*.

S. N. Nwabara is Professor of History and the Director of the Institute of African Studies, University of Nigeria, Nsukka. He received his Ph.D. from Northwestern University and is the author of *Iboland: A Century of Contact with Britain 1860-1960* (London: 1977); and co-author of *A Short History of West Africa A.D. 1000 to the Present*, (London: 1968).

Uzodinma Nwala is a Senior Lecturer in Philosophy at the University of Nigeria, Nsukka. He obtained his Ph.D. from the New School For Social Research in New York and is the author of a novel, *Justice on Trial* (Ibadan: 1973); and *Mbaise in Contemporary Nigeria*, (Gold and Maestro, New York: 1978).

Bode Olowoporoku is a Lecturer in Economics at the University of Ife, Ile-Ife, Nigeria. He received his Ph.D. from Manchester University.

Olayinka Sonaike is a Lecturer in Economics at the University of Ife, Ile-Ife, Nigeria. He received his D. Phil. from Oxford University.

B. C. Sullivan is a Senior Lecturer in International Development Studies at the Polytechnic, Queens Gate, Huddersfield, England. He was formerly a lecturer in Economics at the University of Nigeria, Nsukka. He received his Master of Science (Econs.) from the University of London.

Victor C. Uchendu is Director, African Studies Program and Professor of Anthropology, University of Illinois, Urbana-Champaign. A graduate of the University of Ibadan, Nigeria, he received his Ph.D. from Northwestern University. He was formerly Assistant Professor, Food Research Institute, Stanford University, and has taught at Makerere University, Kampala, Uganda, where he was Director, Makerere Institute of Social Research. Author and co-author of seven books and numerous journal articles, including *The Igbo of Southeast Nigeria* (New York: 1965), *Agricultural Change in Teso, Uganda* (Nairobi: 1974) and *Agricultural Change in Tropical Africa* (Cornell: 1979), Professor Uchendu has also served as President of the African Studies Association of the United States.

# AUTHOR INDEX

# SUBJECT INDEX